Refounding the Church
from the Underside

Refounding the Church from the Underside

ROBERT THORNTON HENDERSON

WIPF & STOCK · Eugene, Oregon

REFOUNDING THE CHURCH FROM THE UNDERSIDE

Copyright © 2011 Robert Thornton Henderson. All rights reserved. Except for brief quotations in critical publications or reviews, no part of this book may be reproduced in any manner without prior written permission from the publisher. Write: Permissions, Wipf and Stock Publishers, 199 W. 8th Ave., Suite 3, Eugene, OR 97401.

Wipf & Stock
An Imprint of Wipf and Stock Publishers
199 W. 8th Ave., Suite 3
Eugene, OR 97401
www.wipfandstock.com

ISBN 13: 978-1-60899-963-7

Manufactured in the U.S.A.

All scripture quotations, unless otherwise indicated, are taken from the English Standard Version (ESV) copyright Crossway Bibles, a division of Good News Publishers of Wheaton, IL. All rights reserved worldwide.

Contents

Foreword: Refounding the Church from the Underside vii
Prologue: The Unfinished Dialogue xi
Introduction: The Questions that Initiated the Journey xxi

Trail Guide #1   Teleology: The Community of the Kingdom of God   1

Trail Guide #2   Cosmology and the Hazards of the Trail   14

Trail Guide #3   Refounding the Church from the Underside   37

Trail Guide #4   Participation, Form, and Character
                 of the Underside Community   44

Trail Guide #5   The Spirit's Formation and Furnishing
                 of the Missional Community   65

Trail Guide #6   Meanwhile . . . Winter is Coming!   95

Epilogue: Vision, Endurance, Faithfulness 107
Bibliography 109

Foreword

Refounding the Church from the Underside

Celebrated novelist Anne Rice recently announced that she was quitting Christianity. An avowed atheist for years, she returned to the faith twelve years ago but is now severing ties with the organized church. "I've been living with this now for 12 years," she told a Los Angeles Times reporter, "and I've come to the conclusion from my experience with organized religion that I have to leave, that I have to, in the name of Christ, step away from this."

Leaving the church in the name of Christ! Sounds preposterous, doesn't it? But listen to her rationale: "It's a matter of rejecting what I've discovered about the persecution of gays, the persecution and oppression of women and the actions of the churches on many different levels. I've also found that I can't find a basis in Scripture for a lot of the positions that churches and denominations take today, and I can't find any basis at all for an anointed, hierarchical priesthood. So all of this finally created a pressure in me, a kind of confusion, a toxic anger at times, and I felt I had to step aside. And that's what I've done."

Note that Anne is not saying that she is rejecting her belief in God as she once did. As a matter of fact, she is quite serious about following the teachings of Jesus. *LA Times* interviewer Mitchell Landsberg was confused: "I wanted to ask you about that," he probed, "because you have said that you quit Christianity 'in the name of Christ.' From a practical standpoint, what does that mean, how do you follow Christ without a church? Are there rituals that you intend to maintain?"

Anne replied: "I think the basic ritual is simply prayer. It's talking to God, putting things in the hands of God, trusting that you're living in God's world and praying for God's guidance. And being absolutely faithful to the core principles of Jesus' teachings."

Rejecting Christianity but not Jesus? Severing ties with the church but not the faith? How can these things be? What has taken place in the institutional church that it is repelling, rather than attracting, conscientious, honorable, and, yes, even spiritual people? On her *Facebook* page, Anne confesses: "I remain committed to Christ as always but not to being 'Christian' or to being part of Christianity. It's simply impossible for me to 'belong' to this quarrelsome, hostile, disputatious, and deservedly infamous group. For ten years, I've tried. I've failed. I'm an outsider. My conscience will allow nothing else."

We might dismiss Anne's decision as one more disgruntled church member at odds with the positions leadership has taken, or as a vocal, strong-minded woman who has an issue with the "maleness" of the religious hierarchy. We might marginalize her decision, treat it as an isolated case, were it not reflective of a widespread societal drift away from denominational church affiliation. Anne's public confession gives voice to the feelings of a generation of young (and not so young) adults who have grown frustrated or bored with the business of organized religion. That is not to say, however, that there is a disinterest in spirituality. Though church membership in the U.S. may be in decline, interest in things spiritual certainly is not. New expressions of spiritual life, like seedlings sprouting from rotting forest nurse logs, are spontaneously springing out of the earth. They may not capture the media attention that towering religious institutions do, but look carefully at ground level and you will discover that the forest floor is green with new growth.

Consider what is currently occurring in our nation's urban centers. For six decades, Christian denominations have withdrawn from the city, following the affluent exodus to the suburbs. Now, with the advent of gentrification, a younger generation of professionals, many faith-motivated, is flooding back into the city. But few are joining the aging churches that still remain. Rather, they are experimenting with new forms of worship and spiritual community. The church-of-the-urban-gentry, more a stirring than a movement at present, is displaying some fresh, very welcome characteristics.

Often spontaneous and informal, these gentry-churches are springing up in non-religious spaces around the city: restaurants, bars, homes and offices. Here, small clusters of spiritually interested young adults meet for fellowship and discussion. Many have no connection to organized religion; some are spawned (or accommodated) by larger "mother" churches or denominations; but most all of them prefer not to identify themselves with denominational names. And while they may not be overtly anti-denominational, they distance themselves from the traditional institutional church's identity, loyalties, and issues. Their management style is participatory, preferring collegiality to top-down appointed leadership. Their orthodoxy tends to be more open than the buttoned-down doctrines of their forebears. Their theology, like their music and rituals, is eclectic. They prefer dialogue to indoctrination, exploration over pedagogy. They love creativity and value intimacy above numerical growth.

To be nuevo-urban is to embrace diversity. And commonly such gentry-churches do—or attempt to. Race, alternative lifestyle, abortion, gender equality—those divisive issues that have splintered the institutional church—find a more charitable climate among the inclusive millennials. Believing that they have grown beyond the prejudices of their parents, the church of Generation Y (born between 1982 and 2003) rejects judgmentalism as small-mindedness. Thus it is a value to have ethnic, class, and cultural diversity in their midst.

The gentry-church is but one sign that the Kingdom is alive and well. The institutional church, as it has been handed down to us, may be undergoing significant and wrenching change, but the church (with a capital C) forges on. As new expressions of the faith continue to spring from the fertile layers of decaying church history, the dichotomy between the Kingdom and the institutional church becomes increasingly obvious. Creating religious institutions is not synonymous with following Jesus. That is why *Refounding the Church from the Underside* is such a timely discussion.

The decline of the Western church is nothing new. All institutions follow a similar pattern. They begin as movements that draw people around an important cause. Life is fresh, energy is abundant, commitment is high, during the movement phase. People are inspired, willing to sacrifice for the mission. There is electricity in the air, a sense that history is being changed, an invitation to have a significant impact on the world.

In time it becomes obvious that in order for the movement to gain traction it must develop some orderly decision making processes. A mission statement must be formulated, leaders must be elected, committees must be created, goals and objectives must be articulated. The organization phase has begun. Staff are hired, a budget is created, an office is opened, governance is established. During this organizational stage, salaries are set and policies and procedures are established. And while progress can now be charted and measurable accomplishments documented, the organization slowly becomes a source of security for its employees. Health insurance, vacation pay, and retirement benefits are negotiated. The cost of living rises. The work load gradually shifts from the founders to hired employees, and with each subsequent layer of management, the passion that originally inspired the movement becomes slightly diluted. A corporate board evaluates the visionary leader(s) and concludes that, though his/her inspiration and zeal were essential in the early stages of the movement, a different skill set is needed to effectively lead the organization forward. A competent CEO is hired. Marketing, management, and funding consume increasing amounts of organizational energy.

By the time the organization enters the institutional phase of its development, it is fully vested in its own self-preservation. Instead of a movement spending itself on behalf of a noble cause, it has become an institution consumed with preserving its own viability and legacy. It may still use the same stirring language of its past movement days, and it may still perform important work, but it spends the lion's share of its funding on buildings, communication systems, staff, and marketing to ensure its longevity. Good stewardship demands it. It is the way of all institutions.

The timeline for progression from movement to institution will be determined by the amount of effort invested in resisting the drift. Experts in organizational theory have differing opinions, but many say forty years is a predictable cycle. One thing is quite certain: the progression is inevitable. In other words, by the time a church is two generations old, its culture has been set, it will be clinging to the security of the familiar, and it will be concerned with its own longevity. Little wonder that a younger generation of progressive, open-minded urbanites find the institutional church unattractive.

Refounding the Church from the Underside offers a portal through which spiritually-interested, church-distanced lay people, young and not so young, can take a glimpse into seldom-visited places in the winding journey of the faith. It is an invitation to exhume the buried layers of rich soil from which, in every generation, new Kingdom growth springs to life. It is a timely challenge for those disenchanted with the present state of the church to re-affirm their place in the unfolding creation drama.

Dr. Robert Lupton
Author
Founder & President of FCS Urban Ministries
Atlanta, Georgia

Prologue

The Unfinished Dialogue

Several years ago, I engaged in a prolonged dialogue with a composite (though not fictitious) friend, to whom I assigned the name "Alan." The dialogue had to do with his questions about the *essence of the church*—like, "*What* in the world is *the church*?" Actually, this composite friend is fashioned out of numerous very real conversations I have had over the table (coffee, lunch, beer—whatever) with several very real, probing, younger minds, who are my friends. So, then, this composite Alan is continually alive and changing as we encounter, together, whole unexplored areas of our lives and thoughts and behaviors as God's New Creation folk—especially as we live together as *church*. These folk know that I struggle, like they struggle, with the whole issue of the integrity of the Christian church scene. And we're certainly not alone! Okay?

That previous dialogue became a book.[1] It recorded the conversation and friendship initiated when (in that literary device, that fabricated dialogue, or whatever you want to call it) this skeptical young inquirer had been given the "full-court press" by the enthusiastic pastor of a large church, who was eager to recruit Alan into *joining* his church institution. Alan was somewhat taken off-guard and not at all convinced that this was anything he wanted to do. So he begged off giving the pastor an answer.

Then, even though we had never formally met, he discovered and recognized me, in the coffee shop of a local bookstore, and somehow discerned me as a fellow-traveler (and someone with credentials) from that same congregation . . . and innocently asked what was my "take" on *the church* in general, and, only secondarily, what was my take on the North Park Church where he had originally met me.

Good questions.

---

1. Robert Thornton Henderson, *Enchanted Community: Journey Into The Mystery Of The Church*.

And so began a two year long conversation in which I had to probe my own heart, mind, convictions, and fifty year background as a pastor and teacher in the Christian community, in order to come up with an answer that was convincing both to Alan and to my own sense of integrity. Our time together dredged up a whole lot of unanswered and conveniently buried questions of my own.

I will not burden you with a review of that conversation. I will, however, commend it to you because of our discussion of "The Signs of Authenticity," which comes near its conclusion.

In the intervening several years, this composite friend (or these several significant conversation partners who make up Alan) have probed me continuously with the next questions, which call forth the considerations that follow. I invite you, my fellow-disciples and readers, to enter into the conversation with us, and weigh critically the perspectives on the church that I am proposing in these pages.

Even as I write this, I am in an ongoing conversation with two gifted and creative young church planters. These guys are dynamically in touch with the urban and generational cultures of our city. They are asking some of the same questions, only from an entirely different cultural perspective. I find their insights and willingness to challenge traditional assumptions most refreshing and helpful. They are quite willing (to borrow a definition) to "suspend the horizons within which everyone else thinks."[2]

But be warned . . . the discussion I am about to initiate here is more than just a mite complex. There are, to be sure, many contradictions and areas of bewildering ambiguity in much of the church as we experience it. Be it known that I am engaging this subject for those—especially my younger friends who are often stumbled by the whole phenomenon of the church—who are willing to think charitably and creatively and critically and prophetically about this subject.

CULTURAL AND ECCLESIASTICAL LIMINALITY

The complexity is exacerbated by the fact that we are in a period of cultural and ecclesiastical *liminality*, i.e., that uncharted transition, from one cultural paradigm to another, for which there are no roadmaps and no guidebooks. To be sure, there are fruitful discussions about the church's

---

2. Gratefully borrowed from Andy Crouch's book *Culture Making*.

self-understanding taking place in movements, and in think tanks, and in missional church gatherings of those who understand this liminality.[3] But... the majority of these discussions are addressed to *church professionals*... and who gets left out in these discussions tends to be all of those *ecclesiastical exiles* (those designated as laity and with whom I identify) who inhabit these *amnesiac* Christendom congregations in this interim cultural whitewater, when all previous patterns of Christian community are in radical transition, refounding, and reconfiguration. We exiles in these congregations somehow identify with the psalmist who sat by the waters of Babylon and wept when he remembered Jerusalem!

Here at the beginning, however, I am compelled to insert, somewhat out of sequence, a very insistent and compelling and interpretive piece to such a trek, to underscore it. That piece has to do with the purpose and intent of the church, in God's design. It will be my basic assumption in what follows that the church is to be *the re-creation of the human community into God's New Creation (or Kingdom of God) demonstration*. The church is to be the re-creation of the human community as God intends it to be... something like that. It is as such that the church is both of the very essence of the gospel and an instrument of that gospel. The church is not ever intended to be a rigid, sterile, comfortable religious institution. I say, then, that our existential context, which I am here addressing, is *liminality* and *exile*. This understanding will permeate all that follows.

The vast church institutions of Christendom bid fair to recede or diminish in significance and prominence in the rapidly emerging future... or perhaps to *morph* into something with a whole different and imaginative missional focus... which we, here and now, would hardly recognize. This all is happening now, and will happen over time, incrementally. The *reality*, of course, is that the western world is populated with untold numbers of traditional Christian institutions, of all stripes, that have long since forgotten who they are, or why they exist, or what they are to be about in God's great design in Christ. Yet within so many of these, perhaps within most of them, there abide, somewhat out of sight, small cohorts of faithful disciples, often discouraged, without ecclesiastical power, and without any faithful *teaching shepherd* to encourage them in living purposefully and fruitfully in that moribund context.

---

3. I would include in this category, at least, the Newbigin syndrome, such as the Gospel And Our Culture Network, along with the emergent church discussions.

So, in addition to my younger friends who are struggling with the whole meaning and integrity of the Christian church, I hope to encourage these fellow exiles in this ecclesiastical liminality—hence, these two target audiences constitute the twofold mission for what follows. My purpose is a hope that I might somehow be a trustworthy and provocative guide—a teaching-shepherd—into a more profound understanding of the church in God's great salvation through Christ. Such a well-intentioned purpose is made the more complex because many of my alienated young friends, as well as many of my fellow exiles in these vast Christendom institutions, who, even while frustrated, or disappointed, or offended by so much of the church phenomenon, still have deep emotional roots and multiple friendships within these same institutions, and so are too attached to them to jump ship and sever relationships.

Such exiles, then, accept, as a significant dimension of their missional calling, that God has *embedded* them within such congregations for a purpose. These are folk who take their baptismal vows to "be Christ's faithful disciple" with earnest intention . . . and yet they live in this tension between their intent and the amnesia of their church institutions. This tension means that we have a whole lot of us who live with a sort of ecclesiastical schizophrenia!

ASKING THE NEEDED QUESTIONS

On the one hand, let us say a person has grown up in the *churchy neighborhood*, where all the rites, words, furnishings, in-house *churchy jargon*, and traditions of the institutional church, in any one of its multiple traditions and forms, are so familiar, that one tends, uncritically, to accept them, and to conform oneself to them without question (mindlessly?) . . . or perhaps to just "chuck them" as irrelevant to his or her life.[4] This *familiar* church expresses the religious dimension of society, and has become part of its social fabric; i.e., it has conformed itself to the dominant social order. On the other hand there are the exiles, who have admitted to themselves that such church institutions are a complicating factor in their Christian discipleship, and have taken a step back . . . and yet wonder how to positively approach the whole reality of God's design for the church.

---

4. I am reminded of the episode reported to me by my friend, an Episcopal rector, of one of his effusive members, who told him, with something of a flourish: "O, I haven't believed in God for years, but I just *love* the Episcopal Church!"

One tends to participate ("join the church") with no expectation of anything of the transformational working of God by the Spirit, and so accepts its reductionist version of the gospel thoughtlessly. The church, then, becomes a *merely human* religious institution. There is little suspicion, among its adherents, of the not-too-remote possibility that it may have little, if anything, to do with what God has done in the event of his Christ . . . or what God intends to do to bless all the people in the world with the wonder of his New Creation!

Such persons would undoubtedly be incredulous at the very suggestion that this familiar church scene might have little, or nothing much at all, to do with the essence of the church Christ purposes to build!

But consider another possibility. What if some happy pagan, some free-spirited postmodern young adult, maybe some *millennial* generation person (or younger), formed by a totally other culture and a different worldview, with an assertive nature and a subliminal spiritual hunger (but with a whole demeanor that is somewhat cynical, humorous, and ruthlessly inquisitive) . . . what if such a person were to approach the threshold of this same neighborhood of *Christendom*,[5] and were to stand there, *de novo*, looking at its pieces, poking around and asking questions, taking nothing at face value . . . and in so doing found that there was quite often, within this *Christendom church*, a distressing unwillingness, by those who are part of it, to critique its own life and activity?

But what if, at the same time, that person also saw many pointers to the fact that, back in there somewhere, somewhere in the church's fading memory, there was a remarkable treasure buried . . . a treasure that is responsible for its beginnings . . . but a treasure long-since having lost its dynamism, forgotten, and essentially consigned to the status of a relic?

All of this might well intrigue such an inquisitive person, and provoke him or her to probe a bit further.

So what is he or she to do?

How does she question the participants? How would he go about discerning if there was any integrity, any real substance? How to find if there is something compelling, something worth pursuing? How would one discern God at work redemptively in such an ecclesiastical scene?

---

5. We'll come back to this in the following discussion, but for now let's define *Christendom* as that self-understanding in which the church has made peace with "the empire" and its dominant social order, and has become identified with the same. It is this understanding that has formed (subverted?) the church for a millennium and a half.

How would such a cynical inquirer discern authenticity in all the religious *stuff* that seems to consume these *churchy institutions*? Or, even more critical, how would such a person come to an engagement with Jesus Christ, by whom and for whom all things exist? Jesus Christ who is the Alpha and Omega of all things? Jesus Christ by whose Name, and none other, we must be rescued, saved? How would such a person be engaged with the transformational power of Jesus Christ? How would he or she see beyond the subversion created by some hyperactive church institution?

Or, maybe . . . consider that there may be others such as I, in my ninth decade of living in just such a churchy neighborhood, who know the profound events which birthed the church two millennia ago. I know something of its history, and even some of the backroads and sidestreets of its historical sojourn in the world, its remarkable accomplishments as well as its periods of unfaithfulness, and its inexcusable embarrassments, and how easily it is distracted. I also know, and I must acknowledge, that whatever it is I am dealing with, I may well, somehow, be walking in the precincts of an awesome mystery, even seeing the footprints of the Holy God. I could become conscious of God's infinite love for the church, whatever that *church* may be, for which he evidently gave his well-beloved Son. I am conscious of all of that, because that's what the New Testament documents affirm.

Having said all of that, I am still frustrated, and maybe angry, at how so much of the life and power and enchantment given to the church by Jesus Christ has been sucked out of it by its seemingly endemic conformity to what might be called the *dominant social order*—and maybe also the dominant ecclesiastical order—so that it has become something far less than God intends it to be. It is, perhaps, a commendable religious institution, with many good works and cultural accomplishments, having nothing to do with the *great eschatological salvation* of God, which was accomplished in Jesus Christ, and for which God intends to incarnate and demonstrate God's New Creation to every people group in the whole earth . . . It is altogether possible that this church phenomenon could even be, even if ever so inadvertently, a contradiction . . . or, as one termed it, a *subversion*.[6]

What if one knows too many family secrets? Or, what if one has asked the ultimate questions . . . and received non-answers?

---

6. See Jacques Ellul, *The Subversion Of Christianity*.

This is not an easy or simple quest. It is far from black and white. The church institutions of Christendom have dominated the scene for at least a millennium and a half . . . Acts of missionary heroism, treasures of music and culture, services faithful and humane, comforts for the suffering, evidences of grace, and more blessings than one can catalog are its legacy. It is an often confusing admixture of "silver and gold and precious stones" along with "wood and hay and stubble."[7] Yet, when that church which is to be the "dwelling place of God by the Holy Spirit"[8] becomes a merely human religious institution, which can only superficially mouth the words of its supernatural character, yet not even expect any expression of the dynamic presence of the spirit of God . . . what are we to conclude? How does the church become so, to say it baldly, *inane*.

Having made such a critical appraisal, it is also true that quite frequently, maybe most frequently, one finds in the most moribund or distracted church institutions an inconspicuous colony of exiles—perhaps not organized in any way, perhaps discouraged, perhaps out of sight, perhaps with no ecclesiastical power—who are serious in their intention to be what they swore in their baptismal vows: "to be Christ's faithful disciple." It is such faithful companies of disciples, dwelling in church institutions that have forgotten their *raison d'être*, that I am designating as *The Church From the Underside*. What follows, then, is both for my inquisitive younger friends, and also for that underside community: they are actually on the same quest.

ILLUSTRATION: HIKING THE APPALACIAN TRAIL

Like I say . . . it's complex. But let's plunge in. Let me explain what I intend to do by way of an illustration. A couple of years ago, my young friend Jennifer decided that she would celebrate completion of her college career by hiking the whole Appalachian Trail from Georgia to Maine. To do this she didn't just hoist her back pack one day and take off for the beginning of the trail in north Georgia. Not at all. Rather, over the decades, scores of others who walked that trail before her had written guides spelling out the landscape, the hazards, the weather possibilities, the physical demands, the provisions along the trail, the markers posted

---

7. 1 Cor 3:12.
8. Eph 2:22.

along the trail at given mile points, the organizations which exist to help the hikers, and so much more.

Jennifer knew the physical conditioning required and the equipment necessary in order to fulfill her quest. With such conditioning and information, she began the trek. Over several months, she posted reports from the trail whenever she could find an internet connection, so that I and others could share vicariously the experience with her. Her reports revealed aspects of the trail that I could never have imagined. The happy ending is that, though she encountered ecstatic moments, and horrendous weather, and made marvelous friendships—even had the nightmarish moment of stumbling upon a suicide—she ultimately arrived in Maine, with a sense of accomplishment and celebration.

Our journey into being the *underside church* requires no less preparation and conditioning, and will result in experiences both ecstatic and traumatic. It will also bring us into contact with others with similar convictions about Christ's design for the community of his disciples.

INITIATING THE JOURNEY

I want to initiate a journey into the possibility of *refounding* the church from the underside. If I, in these pages, can put together some *trail markers* for this quest, shared by so many of us who are exiles in the church, what would it need to include, in order to be useful to fellow exiles in their engagement with such amnesiac church institutions? And, let me assure my readers that, before all of these reflections, it is my intended purpose to *encourage* the exiles—to be positive. Whether I succeed or not remains to be seen.[9]

It doesn't help us to be frozen in passive dissatisfaction with the church's forgetfulness, or with its displaced *raison d'être*. Rather, it is for us to become, ourselves, salt and light. At the very least we can become gentle evangelists within that particular church community where we are in exile (or where we join the other exiles as an inquirer!). In so doing, we become *the church from the underside*, that subversive movement

---

9. I confess that this is probably a totally insane project since it requires something of a redefinition of the church. It will not compute with those who are traditionalists. It will always be in process and will never be in any final or even near-perfect form. I offer it only as a provocation for discussion, and for exploration into the missional design so obvious in New Testament documents. It has been gestating in my psyche during the whole of my fifty year career as a teacher in the realities of the church's congregational life.

embedded within the *Christendom church* communities. As audacious as it sounds, we might well become missionaries to, and within, these very church communities.

My purpose here is to attempt to provide a sense of purpose, a sense of meaning, a sense of mission, for those of us whose lot is to be part of the somewhat anonymous, but leavening colony of exiles—the underside churches—that inhabit a large number of traditional Christendom churches of all stripes. We are not really free to do anything other than seek to be faithful agents of the Spirit of God in these far-from-convincing congregations. Exiles!

And if, in this journey, I can also encourage an emerging generation of ecclesiastical skeptics to become part of God's mission, then I am doubly fulfilled.

Join me, then, as we continue the ongoing conversation. And let me note here that I have put some significant references and enhancements in my footnotes, and encourage my readers to access them.

Introduction

The Questions that Initiated the Journey

ALAN AND I HAD landed for the first time in many months at a little offbeat coffee house across College Avenue from the train tracks. We were seated at a table on the sidewalk on a pleasantly warm summer morning. We almost had to become reacquainted, since we had been out of communication for so long. It had been several years since Alan and I had first grappled at-length with the whole issue of the nature of the church, and of whether or not he should respond to the invitation to join North Park Church. We had rather agreed at that time that there were probably sufficient signs of *authenticity* in the North Park scene to warrant his taking the plunge, and so he had.

We had ordered our coffee and bagels, and then he hadn't wasted any time with niceties. First off, daily life for him had become quite difficult since he was one of the victims of the current economic recession, and the company he was with was struggling. Unemployment loomed as a real possibility. The issues of life inescapably color one's appraisal of one's experience in such a community as the Christian church. But his circumstances at the moment weren't what were on his mind. He launched right in.

THE QUESTIONS

"Okay, Bob, now that I've spent all of these months as part of North Park Church, with your encouragement, mind you—I'm not blaming you by the way—I'm having more questions than ever about the church. I have a really tough time finding anybody in North Park who really knows why the church even exists in the first place—or who seems to care. I mean: 'Why is the church?' That would seem like an obvious and basic question, wouldn't it? But most seem surprised that I should even ask the question. How in the hell did a church with such an orthodox history and institutional hubris, as North Park professes to have, ever get this out-of-it? And what in the

world does one do with such amnesia, positively? I mean, I haven't got the slightest interest in leaving North Park. S'matter of fact, I'm really irrationally attached to it. But, then, I don't know why in the world I want to stay with it either. The whole scene is an enigma to me.

"Maybe it is not too excessive to say that it totally exasperates me—but then that's why I'm on your doorstep here. I need to vent. If I am honest, I find North Park—and other church scenes I have been exposed to—to be, maybe, superficial, dishonest, detached from reality and irrelevant to my life, embarrassingly mindless, and with so much wasted potential."

At this point I had to grin and interject: "But apart from all of that you have nothing but good things to say about it, right?"

"Okay, wise guy, I know I'm being a bit negative. But . . . there are those remnants of authenticity that you and I have talked about. There are all of those other friends, who, like me, like us, share in the hope of a more authentic expression of 'New Creation reality' emerging somehow in that scene.

"So tell me, do I just hunker down and die of boredom or frustration—or mindless passivity—or are there some disciplines, other options, or understanding or anointing, that can incarnate God's purpose in Christ for the church—whatever that might be—with integrity . . . or, to use that word again, authenticity?

"If I had a friend searching for God, North Park is the last place I'd suggest he or she look!"

ASSUMPTIONS ABOUT THE CHURCH, GOOD AND BAD

I record this piece of our conversation because I think it's important for us to know what people honestly think about the church—both good and bad. Many people have assumptions about God that are bad, which color their whole ability to respond to any invitation to Christian faith. We need to know what those assumptions are so that we can deal with them. So, also, many people have experiences and assumptions about the church that are bad, and which affect their ability to know how to respond to it. It really doesn't help us to deny these experiences and assumptions. Alan needed to vent. His honesty in dumping all this on me is really quite necessary. It's part of the process of finding our way out of this.

The Barna Research Group has reported something like twenty million "born again Christians" who don't even participate in any church since they find it irrelevant to their lives. "Dropping out" is an option, but I really don't think it's at all a viable one. That said, I take Alan's disenchantment with the church seriously, and make it my point of entrance to some guides and proposals that have the practical and redemptive potential of *refounding the church from the underside* (the explanation of that phrase will unfold along the way).

We need to look, initially, at what our options are:

FIVE OPTIONS

1. *Drop out.* This is may be the path of least resistance, but it is not at all acceptable. The New Testament documents make our responsibility to one another within a community of disciples a *sine qua non* of Christian discipleship. By our baptism we become part of God's design to recreate the human community into its true and eschatological[10] design.

2. *Become part of, or engage in, a new church "plant."* Planting new churches is essential to the mission of God to get the gospel to every corner of the human community. However, it should absolutely *not* be for the purpose of giving refuge to rootless and demanding dissidents, and ecclesiastical vagabonds, from other churches. The purpose of planting new churches is to incarnate the gospel in those places—neighborhoods, villages, definable areas of need, etc.—where there is that darkness that needs the presence of the light of God's New Creation in Christ. The purpose should also be incarnational, i.e., the gospel on display in a neighborhood. This means that those who are integral to the new church should live in that context, not be commuters. Planting a new church is a demanding missional responsibility, and needs well-informed and well-equipped initiators, who demonstrate the New Creation they are talking about.

3. *Become a "church shopper"*—moving from church to church looking for a more congenial and less demanding setting . . . or a more inspiring preacher. This is the most immature and frequent response for all too many of those who profess to be Christ's disciples. It totally absolves one from any of the relational responsibilities of being God's New Creation folk.

---

10. *Eschatological* is a great word, and you can check it out on Wikipedia!

4. *Stay where you are and become the resident critics* and contrarians, subjecting everything to your own merely human appraisal, with no redemptive vision, and so never making any positive contribution, to what God would design, for his own glory, in that wilderness often of sterility and forgetfulness.

5. *Accept the vision of refounding the church from the underside* as a Spirit-given mission to create, right in the midst of this ecclesiastical wasteland, a "beautiful bride for the Lamb" . . . to create an incarnation of New Creation community, in accordance with scripture, in which God's purpose in Christ is on display where you are. I would give an initial definition of *underside church* as something like a critical mass of self-effacing disciples who find themselves in similar amnesiac church institutions as Alan's, who understand the teleology of the church and its role in the mission of God, and who sense their own calling to demonstrate their discipleship, in that very place, for the blessing of others and the fulfillment of the mission of God. Such cohorts of disciples are quite willing to fly under the radar, i.e., be *hidden*, and so be of no special importance—always with the vision and hope of being those leavening and transformational blessings within the larger community by the Spirit of God.

What follows will describe the journey into incarnating this fifth option—the wholesome formation of a New Creation community within the larger ecclesiastical scene . . . an underside church that is authentically focused on God's purpose of creating such a beautiful bride for the Lamb of God.[11] This means that, before we even begin this journey, I need to insist that what I am about to propose is intended to be an act of worship. Even though I will propose some rather unusual and even radical visions, and even though I may attempt to remove some of the horizons that have defined the church classically, I do it out of a heart that passionately seeks God's "glory in the church and in Christ Jesus."[12] It is certainly not intended for the grumpy dissidents who inhabit many

---

11. A number of authors such as Paul Bilheimer have employed this description of God the Father's purpose in the church. It is a community that is so conformed to the image of the Son that it becomes that intimate fulfillment that a bride is to her husband. Think about it!

12. Eph 3:21.

churches with their unhappiness, like a dark cloud, bringing negativism and discouragement in their wake.

This is not as simple as it may sound. There are many inter-animating themes that define each other as we go along. Two of these, right up front, are 1) the necessity of understanding the teleology of the church, and 2) the necessity of understanding the dominance of the *gospel of the Kingdom of God* theme in the New Testament. But, before we even approach these two in Trail Guide # 1, we need to agree that our first motivation is doxological—the church is to be the community of the glory of God. It is the glory of the Triune God, whose church it is. That is our motivation in what follows.[13] Okay?

---

13. 2 Cor 8:23; Ephesians 3:21.

Trail Guide #1

Teleology: The Community of the Kindgom of God

Let's tackle the first big question: *Why* is the church? At the very trailhead of any journey, it only makes sense to know where in the world this adventure is taking you. We absolutely need to know the purpose and the destination of the path we are setting out on. It is no less critical when we initiate our journey into such a mission as that of *Refounding the Church from the Underside*.[1]

With such a journey, as we have set ourselves to explore, come some immediate questions needing clarification, not to mention some of those inter-animating themes that we mentioned earlier. So, here's what I want to do: First, I want to explore the church and its purpose. Secondly, I think we must look carefully at who are the component persons making up the church, which will bring us to the critical area of *discipleship*; and then, thirdly, I want to tie both of these inextricably to the major theme of the New Testament, which is the gospel of the Kingdom of God.

Let's begin then with our need for some clarity of meaning about the very word *church*, which we tend to use somewhat mindlessly. What in the world is the *church*? The word is not at all an explicitly Christian word. Rather, it is a borrowed Greek word: *ek-klesia* (called out). It pertains to an assembly of folk *called out* for a purpose, perhaps political, civil, religious, or other. Jesus employed the word in his moment of messianic self-affirmation at Caesarea Philippi,[2] but then he never even defined what he was talking about—only that whatever it was, it would

---

1. *Refounding* is the word I am deliberately employing. I have borrowed it from several provocative books by Gerald Arbuckle of the Marynoll Order. His conviction is that "renewal" and "revival" are far too weak when seeking to return a church (or in his case, a Roman Catholic order) to its "founding myth," i.e., that original set of principles, values, and purpose that created it in the first place. I will return to this along the journey.

2. Matt 13:18.

be of his own building. Its completion would be a divine certainty. Since he didn't even stop to define what he was talking about, all we know is that Jesus intended to call out a people who would somehow be agents of this selfsame ministry in which he, himself, had been anointed by God.

Which would necessarily lead us to two further questions: *called out of what*? And, then, *called into what*—and for what purpose?

These two questions bring us then to the discipline of *teleology*. The next question might be: what would such an assembly of called-out people look like, and what would they do to fulfill whatever it was that Jesus was calling them for? But note: this implies at least two other initially un-named *cosmic* realities: one would be that cosmic reality *out of* which this community is called . . . and the other would be that cosmic—or eschatological—reality *into which* it is called. We'll be coming back to that again and again, because, as we'll find, they are inimical to each other and in ultimate conflict . . . and so need to be very clearly defined in our minds if we are to accomplish the purpose of our journey.

TELEOLOGY

But let's begin with *teleology*:[3] Now there's a good word for you.

As we insisted above, initiating any journey should involve having some deliberate sense of the purpose and the destination, some sense of the *teleology* of the journey. It would be a bit ingenuous for us to even begin to talk about the church if we had no clue as to why it existed in the heart and mind of God. To that end, we will need to be looking for some sense of this meaning concerning our calling to be part of that awesome mystery known as Christ's church . . . then we desperately need also that overarching understanding of what God in Christ has in mind in building his church. We need to know how the church is, somehow, of the essence of the gospel—that joyous announcement of God.

When, perhaps, our present *merely human*[4] church institutions do not have such a deliberate self-consciousness, it is even more incumbent

---

3. *Teleology*: "The fact or character of being directed toward an end or shaped by a purpose—used of natural processes or of nature as a whole conceived as determined by final causes or by the design of a divine Providence and opposed to purely mechanical determinism . . ." (*Webster's Third New International Dictionary*).

4. I employ this translation of a Greek word variously rendered as *carnal*, or *flesh*, or *without Spirit*. What it connotes is that which is part of the creation alienated from God and so devoid of God's indwelling.

upon (what I am designating as) the *underside church* itself to have its own very clear and self-conscious teleology of the church—or maybe even more basically—to have a very clear *ecclesiology*. Such a clear sense of ecclesiology is a *sine qua non* of our intention to be the underside church with any integrity. Shortly, we shall seek to put a little clearer definition on what I am designating here as *the underside church*.

Let me invoke an illustration from J. R. R. Tolkien's epic: *The Lord of the Rings*. In that story, Frodo Baggins and Sam Gamgee were two "hobbits" who were the key figures in a mythic adventure. They always felt terribly inadequate to the task which they had been assigned. Many times they did not know exactly where they were in their journey, and in their quest to destroy the ring of power. They often doubted their own ability to even carry out the task . . . but for all of their weaknesses and self-doubt they did, in fact, always know and remember what were their purpose and their destination.

They knew it was critical for them to somehow arrive at their destination, which was Mt. Doom. There they were to destroy the ominous ring of power, with all of its cosmically destructive potential. They were well aware of how ultimate was their task, if they were to preserve Middle Earth and the bucolic way of life, in which they had previously prospered, in their homeplace, known as "the Shire." They knew that such was their *purpose* because they had been so mandated by the authoritative Council of Elrond.[5] Clear to them were both the teleology of their journey and an understanding of the conflict it would involve.

Let's begin, then, with a "*You Are Here!*" bit of self-location. You will recognize this note of orientation from many trail maps (or shopping mall visitor guides). We *exiles*, in our present, existential, institutional, frequently forgetful, and very real local churches, are where we are—we are not somewhere else, or in some other setting. In one sense, we are where no one else has ever been before, and yet . . . in another sense, we are where a great host of Christ's people has been, in very similar circumstances, from the very beginnings of the church. This moment, this place, these circumstances, this culture are our "trail." It is the place of our incarnation of the gospel. This is the locus of our exile and of our journey in the mission of God.

---

5. Apologies to my "culturally deprived" friends who have never read J. R. R. Tolkein's marvelous saga *The Lord Of The Rings*.

You and I live in a *here and now* relationship, or non-relationship, to any one—or more—of the specific expressions, or forms, of what pertains to be the church. These can range anywhere from clandestine house churches to moribund denominational franchises, or to vibrant assemblies of Kingdom dynamism, or from small committed communities to the vast formal institutional expressions of the Christendom era, or to excited new church plants—or none of the above. But in whatever form, the church exists in some visible "wineskin"—some form of community that assembles in some place and at some time.

This being so, it stands to reason that, at the very beginning of such a journey as ours, toward an understanding of our mission to and within such churches, it doesn't make a great deal of sense for us to begin without some sense of the purpose, some sense of the destination, some teleology of the church.[6] Like: what is it that our Creator God has in mind for his people who are called "the church"? The answer to that question is especially incumbent upon those of us who identify ourselves as the underside church. After all, this entity called the church carries with it some awesome Biblical descriptions: the bride of Christ, the Body of Christ, and the dwelling place of God by the Spirit . . . for starts.

Be it known that a gathering of sociable religious folk, milling about in some *churchy neighborhood*—whether it be a venerable old Christendom institution, or some experimental new church plant meeting in the park—doesn't necessarily indicate the integrity of that community as a true church.[7] The form doesn't guarantee that many (if any) of them have much notion of God's purpose for the church. There are probably many commendable and attractive components, as well as cautioning problems, present in whatever form. Nor does it necessarily follow that such folk have much of an articulate notion of what their own particular life has to do with any understanding of Christ calling out a people that they might demonstrate to others what God's human community, recreated in Christ, looks like.

---

6. If we do not have such a sense of purpose and destination, then we become like the lyrics of the old drinking song: "We're here, because we're here, because we're here." Nothing more. And tragically that's where many church folk spend their lives.

7. Annie Dillard ruminates on this theme in her book *Teaching A Stone To Talk*. She asks: "Why do we people in churches seem like cheerful, brainless tourists on a packaged tour of the Absolute? The tourists are having coffee and doughnuts on Deck C. Presumably someone is minding the ship, correcting the course, avoiding icebergs and shoals, . . . Does anyone have the foggiest idea what sort of power we so blithely invoke?" (*Teaching A Stone*, 40).

It would be inconceivable to most *traditional church folk* that the church is actually to be the human community God intended it to be in creation and which was totally defiled by the rebellion of our first human parents. The church, then, is the true human community, which God is now recreating through his Son . . . with all of the communal dimensions of that *New Creation*, including a supernatural indwelling by the Spirit. These same well-intentioned, traditional, church folk might be taken aback to know that a plethora of attractive and commendable church activities may well indicate something quite irrelevant of, alien to, subversive of, or even oblivious to the mission of the reign of God.

So what is the teleology of Christ's church?

First off, the church would need to know and be formed, in its communal life, by its purpose in the heart and mind of God. Such purpose can only be discerned from the biblical documents. Questions immediately arise: 1) *Why* is the church? 2) *What* is it designed to be, and do, and think, in the purpose of God? 3) *How* do I understand, and fit into, such a design? 4.) *How* am I to be a faithful and fruitful part of God's mission as expressed in the church?

THE DOMINANT THEME:
THE GOSPEL OF THE KINGDOM OF GOD

In order to comprehend the church's teleology, we need to be alerted here, at the outset, to another dominant and insistent piece of our Biblical landscape: namely, *the gospel of the Kingdom of God*. Let me explain why I insist on this as a priority, and a most critical consideration, for our mission of refounding the church from the underside . . . not to mention our understanding something of what this called-out community, this church, is called into.

Living, as I have, for a long time, in the midst of this ecclesiastical culture, I have had the sense that there has been, all too frequently, something missing in answers to these critical questions—something just didn't connect. I sense it when I hear otherwise gifted church leaders and clergy totally miss the point of key texts having to do with the awesomeness of what God came to accomplish in Christ. I miss it in so much of the material about the disciplines of *spirituality*. I miss it in many of the missiological studies in which I have been engaged. But what that something missing *is* has been one of those mysteries that have too often fairly eluded me, one that I have not been able to articulate or put my finger on.

Then an epiphany! In an unexpected moment, I had a really outrageous thought . . . and yet so compelling.

I was sitting at a stoplight on Scott Boulevard. I was listening to a taped discussion between an interviewer and a literary historian. The question came: Is it possible for a literary critic who is totally unfamiliar with the dominant influence which Christian theology has so profoundly exercised on the culture of the period in which a piece of literature was written, and on the author, . . . to criticize with any integrity such a work as Dante's *Inferno* (which these two were discussing)?

The answer was obviously "No!" He or she could not—not with any integrity. Yet so many who are formed by a secular culture, and an accompanying biblical illiteracy, have tried. Otherwise quite gifted academicians do not have eyes to see the role and influence of the whole Christian culture, which has so significantly influenced much of the great literature of the past and present. How, then, could anyone appreciate such literature without the knowledge and worldview and Biblical heritage that formed and informed the author, for whom it was all so presuppositional?

Then, my epiphany!

My mind made a leap: If the clearly dominant theme of so much of the New Testament has to do with the gospel of the Kingdom of God, which it unmistakably has, especially obvious in the synoptic gospels . . . if that which was the primary theme of Jesus' public preaching . . . if that same compelling message is what Paul concluded his life preaching, while in captivity in Rome, at the risk of his life, right under the noses of the ostentatious power of another dominion, namely the hostile Roman Empire . . . if that awesome cosmic and eschatological theme is what dominates the whole of the New Testament, and has been inadvertently *displaced, diluted*, or *forgotten*[8] by a frighteningly large portion of our present church establishment . . . then it is not at all surprising that our understanding of Christ's church, its form and its message, is also reduced, or at least truncated, to something much, much less than the divine intention—maybe even to something that might be described as *chaos*!

On the face of it, *the church is somehow to be the communal demonstration of the Kingdom of God.*[9]

---

8. Once again I give credit for these descriptions here to Gerald Arbuckle, especially his *Out Of Chaos* and *Refounding The Church*.

9. I will use the terms Kingdom of God, and New Creation somewhat interchange-

The divine intention is obviously that the church is to be the human community recreated into its divinely intended essence, i.e., the recreated human community—*the community of the Kingdom of God* (provisionally)—invested with the divine nature by the dynamic presence of the Holy Spirit. That divine intention is that the church *be the flesh and blood demonstration of God's New Creation in its communal form.* The divine intention is that the church is to be, like Christ, *the missionary arm of the Trinity* by which God's blessing is communicated to every people group on earth. It is to be the primary agent of God's great search-and-rescue-mission in Christ. And ultimately the divine intention is that God the Father is preparing, by the church, a *beautiful bride for the Lamb of God.*

Those four facets, at the very least, give us some conception of the teleology of the church:

1. *The community of the Kingdom of God* (provisionally).
2. *The flesh and blood demonstration of God's Kingdom, or New Creation, in its communal form.*
3. *The missionary arm of the trinitarian community.*
4. *A beautiful bride for the Lamb.*

Minus these critical dimensions of the divine teleology the church is reduced to something much, much less than what is presented us in the New Testament documents! When it is so reduced, then, it cannot fulfill its calling by Christ, which calling is to demonstrate, before the watching world, the *human community as God intends it to be* in all of its transformational New Creation, or Kingdom of God, presence. When it is so reduced or truncated, it exhibits not much more than simply one more merely human religious institution.

With that kind of reductionism, the church becomes completely explainable in merely human terms. There is nothing supernatural about it. It certainly cannot become that community, formed by the Spirit of the Father and the Son, with the purpose of incarnating the reality of its Redeemer, who by the Spirit's indwelling "*is able to do far more abundantly*

---

ably. There are several familiar designations of God's great eschatological design that are near synonymous in the New Testament: Kingdom of God, New Creation, Eternal Life, Salvation, the Age to Come, sometimes the term Righteousness is used in this way, and there are probably some others. All refer to God's purpose to make all things new through Christ.

than all that we ask or think, according to the power at work within us, to him be glory in the church and in Christ Jesus throughout all generations."[10]

It is almost laughable to even consider that such a forgetful church could ever be the bearer of God's thrilling announcement of the dawn of *all things new* through his Messiah (Anointed One)—for such is the meaning of the word *gospel* (which word means *thrilling news*, or *joyous announcement*, in its Greek roots). So much of the church in which I have lived has been anything *but* the contagious community demonstrating such a joyous New Creation reality in flesh and blood reality.

From that moment at that stoplight—and even as the light turned green—things began to make sense. Pieces began to fall into place. Even the ostensibly evangelical church of my own habitation has essentially forgotten, or truncated, the biblical proportions and the thrilling dimensions of the gospel. We are, in reality, in danger of becoming an almost *gospel-less church*, by any New Testament definition.

Like the church at Galatia, we, the church, over the generations, have tailored the gospel downward to fit our own less-than-biblical definitions and expectations of what Jesus was all about—and so what we have created is a subjectivized, humanly-focused bit of good news defined in mostly personal dimensions—sort of a *designer gospel*.[11] We have taken God's love, God's patience and kindness, God's forgiveness, and our adoption through Jesus Christ—as true and deserving of our adoration as those pieces of the gospel are—and made them to be the whole of it, with no discernable relationship to the great all-encompassing eschatological Kingdom of God (or God's New Creation in Christ).

To raise such a critical evaluation is not even to mention that we have also tended to *redefine* the Kingdom of God in all kinds of clever and subjective, or dualistic, or escapist, or *spiritual* ways that are inimical to its biblical proportions. Not only is the gospel of the Kingdom of God the primary and dominant designation of God's thrilling announcement at the coming of Christ . . .

But . . . but . . . the gospel of the Kingdom of God is *big!*
The gospel of the Kingdom is a huge and all embracing concept.
The gospel of the Kingdom is awesome.
The gospel of the Kingdom is cosmic.

---

10. Eph 3:20–21, ESV.

11. I think it was N. T. Wright who observed that what passed for worship and preaching in many contemporary churches was nothing less than "therapeutic deism." Others have termed it "MTD," or "moralistic, therapeutic deism."

The gospel of the Kingdom speaks in near-synonymous terms of the same eschatological reality as other New Testament terms such as *salvation*, such as *the age to come*, such as *eternal life*, such as *New Creation* . . . and often, most probably, other terms, such as *righteousness*. As I say, a substantial case can be made that these are all near-synonymous designations of the same reality.

The gospel of the Kingdom is holistic, in that it cannot be confined to human definitions of *religion* or *spirituality* that are cloistered away from every other dimension of God's creation, what with all of its beauty and glory on one hand . . . and its ugliness, rebellion, and tragedy on the other.

The gospel of the Kingdom is radically and profoundly incarnational in this present world, which world is the scene of a cosmic rebellion against its Creator (we will spell this out more carefully in the next Trail Guide).

The gospel of the Kingdom is—if I may employ this accurate, but not too familiar term—eschatological,[12] in that it speaks of God's ultimate and end-times purpose of incarnating the reign of God. It speaks of God's purpose of reconciling the world to himself, and of destroying Satan and the dominion of darkness. This eschatological Kingdom of God was inaugurated with the coming of Jesus Christ, and by his cross—but its inauguration points to the day when this divine purpose, this gospel of the Kingdom, shall have been heralded in all the earth for a witness. This means, then, that the gospel of the Kingdom always has a future-focused, or eschatological, dimension in which this already inaugurated *dominion of God's son* will be ultimately consummated, and in which God becomes all, and in all, to his whole creation . . . while at the same time being dynamically present here and now by the Holy Spirit.[13]

The gospel of the Kingdom is God's personal entry into his own rebellious creation in the flesh and blood person of his son Jesus Christ, in order to make all things new.

The gospel of the Kingdom is even bigger than that. It takes very seriously the reality, the presence, and the destructive and blighting malice, of Satan, who is the devil, in all the affairs of humankind! "The

---

12. *Eschatological*: "*adj*: of, relating to, dealing with, or as regards to the ultimate destiny of mankind and the world" (*Webster's New Third International Dictionary*).

13. This is frequently expressed as "the-already-but-not-yet-Kingdom of God."

reason the Son of God appeared was to destroy the works of the devil,"[14] or, in the words of Isaac Watts's hymn: "He comes to make his blessings flow far as the curse if found."[15]

The gospel of the Kingdom is validated by the cross, on which Jesus "disarmed the rulers and authorities and put them to open shame, by triumphing over them in him."[16] For this compelling reason the preaching of the cross is critical to the church's integrity and power.

This *gospel of the Kingdom* is: "Grace be to you and peace from God our Father and the Lord Jesus Christ, who gave himself for our sins to deliver us from the present evil age, according to the will of God and Father . . ."[17] This word was written to a church that had begun tailoring (reducing?) the gospel of the Kingdom of God to fit, and to be non-confrontational with, its ethnically Hebrew proponents, and so to miss the divine purpose in which all of creation is to be blessed in Jesus Christ.

The gospel of the Kingdom always places our personal deliverance from sin, and from this present evil age, in the larger context of God's design to redeem his fallen and rebellious creation *in toto*—"Behold, I make all things new."[18]

The gospel of the Kingdom brings into flesh and blood reality—and within the human experience—the very divine will and nature. The eschatological design of God does not exist in some ethereal and spiritual *never-never-land* of unreality. Rather, it dynamically invades this present human community by the veritable incarnation of that divine will and character, even as it becomes spelled out in the Spirit-inhabited lives of Christ's followers, formed by the teachings of Jesus, such as the Sermon on the Mount. This means that people observing may *look* and *see* the glory of God lived out in true human community by the power of God: ". . . *that men may see your good works* [i.e., your Kingdom thinking and behavior] *and give glory to your Father who is heaven.*"[19]

---

14. 1 John 3:8. Trying to conceive of the gospel without this cosmic warfare with the prince of darkness is like trying to tell the story of the *Lord of the Rings* without mentioning the one ring of power, or the presence of Sauron in Middle Earth in the *Rings* trilogy of J. R. R. Tolkein.

15. From the Advent hymn "Joy to the World."

16. Col 2:15.

17. Gal 1:3–4.

18. Rev 21:5.

19. Matt 5:16.

BACK TO TEOLOGY

Since the gospel of the Kingdom of God is at the heart of Jesus' teaching, be it known that it also brings with it a very insistent *communal dimension*. It is this communal dimension that informs our quest after the church's teleology, absolutely. The Kingdom of God is, among other things, God's thrilling design in Christ to recreate the human community, and its internal relationships, in order to reflect God's own character and purpose. In its communal expression, the church is to reflect the relationship that exists between the persons of the Trinity—what is called by theologians the *perichoresis* of the trinitarian community.[20] "By this shall all people know that you are my disciples if you have love for one another." "As the Father has loved me, so have I loved you . . ."[21] The church is the thrilling reconstitution of the true human community in the embrace of the divine (trinitarian) community.

The gospel of the Kingdom is also inescapably personal. We come as part of the cosmic rebellion, with all of our brokenness and guilt and missing-the-point of the true purpose of our human lives. This gospel meets us in all of our unique individuality, and with our capacities and needs, but the gospel has a divine intention to make us those persons in whom God dwells by his own Spirit. The purpose of the gospel is to demonstrate what is *true humanity* in us, individually and communally. We are reconciled, forgiven, and adopted—and, ultimately, gifted . . . and in process of being "conformed to the image of God's Son."[22]

Having said that, however, the gospel of the Kingdom is much, much more than *my personal salvation*. It is that, no question . . . but it is so much more. The community of the Kingdom of God is made up of those rescued from darkness and translated into the Kingdom of God's dear son.[23] But it is much more than personal spiritual therapy. It is a calling into a radical and subversive, wholly new way of thinking and living into God's New Creation, which is the glory of God. The gospel of the Kingdom is, if anything, *counter-cultural*.

---

20. This is so beautifully expressed in Samuel Stone's hymn "The Church's One Foundation": "Yet she on earth hath union / With God the Three in One . . ."

21. John 13:35; 15:9.

22. Rom 8:28–30. This is one of the most misused passages that I know of in that speakers will regularly take the first part about all things working for good, but will fail to go on to the design of this work of God which is to conform us to the image of Christ.

23. Col 1:13.

The gospel of the Kingdom is a message and a reality that must, of necessity, always stand in "missionary confrontation" (to use Lesslie Newbigin's term)[24] with the dominion of darkness—with this present world—into which it comes redemptively. Thus it is radically transformational, and cannot be conformed to this present evil age. It is, as I have written elsewhere, by its very *raison d'être,* "radical and subversive."[25]

There is one door into this New Creation, into this dominion of God's dear son, into this Kingdom community, and that door is Jesus Christ alone. Only through Christ do we enter into communion with the Triune God.

. . . Enough for now, but this is, I hope, to make graphic before you that the church is to be the communal dimension and demonstration of that Kingdom of God. It is to be that veritable community of God's New Creation in Christ. It is provisionally so. It is in process of being conformed to the image of God's son. It is always a community of aliens and exiles. But, even so, it is always to be a critical component of God's thrilling announcement in Christ: the Gospel. Which component, then, brings us to our dilemma. It also brings us to my own motivation in putting this into writing, which is to assist my fellow exiles in creating authentic colonies of Kingdom authenticity, underside churches, to serve quietly as light and leaven in larger institutional expressions of the church that have far too often forgotten, diluted, or displaced their teleology!

SPECIFICS FOR THE TRAIL

Underside Churches have no specific form. They are clusters, or networks, or fellowships, of those intentional followers of Christ who are mutually supporting, inter-animating, and in responsible-accountable relationship with each other. These small cohorts of Christ's followers share a very clear *Kingdom consciousness,* or a very clear sense of divine teleology for the church, and deliberately and regularly remind each other of this calling. They eschew any quest for power. They are

---

24. Don't ask me where Newbigin uses it, but probably in *The Gospel In A Pluralist Society.* At least I attribute it to him.

25. Henderson, *Enchanted Community,* 158.

content to be out-of-sight, or hidden, but mutually share a vision for the larger ecclesiastical scene, and a responsibility to be servants as the Spirit gives them gifts and occasions to minister in love and humility. Such underside communities have existed throughout the church's history, and especially in times of the larger church's unfaithfulness. They meet around tables, they pray, they love and serve, they nurture and reinforce each other in their mutual role as salt and light in the midst of the larger community. I write these Trail Guides for the exiles in what will later be described as the larger, impersonal, and often amnesiac Christendom church institutions. However, these same Trail Guides could easily also be founding principles for new church planting, or nurturing lessons on ecclesiology.

Trail Guide #2

Cosmology and the Hazards of the Trail

Be it known that such a journey as we are proposing here is not likely to be always a pleasant, or even a safe, trek through neutral territory. Nor is the trail always plainly marked. There will always be fog, forks in the trail, misplaced trail markers, darkness, and a myriad of hazards—not to mention "near thee lurks the evil one"[1]—to keep us from our God-given destination. Let me explain. When Alan asks, "How in the hell did a church with such an orthodox history and institutional hubris, as North Park professes to have, ever get this out-of-it?" such a question could not be more appropriate.

How did it? How does the church so often get so out-of-it? What are the dynamics that so subtly cause such a professed church community to become something quite other than what it was originally intended to be? How does forgetfulness set in? What are the seductions? Or, more in tune with our hiking metaphor, what are the false trails that take us where we never intended, originally, to go?

Such inquiry brings us to our second big question: What is the realistic context of our calling to be God's New Creation community? What's the bigger picture?

For starts, it is worth going back to Jesus' affirmation of his eschatological mission as God's Anointed One (or *Messiah*, or *Christ*) in accomplishing God's great salvation. In response to Jesus' question to the twelve at Caesarea Philippi—"Who do you say that I am?"—Peter had confessed: "You are the Christ, the Son of the Living God." Jesus immediately and unequivocally responded that Peter's affirmation was God-given.

---

1. From Charlotte Elliott's nineteenth century hymn, "Christian, Seek Not Yet Repose."

Then, note carefully: Jesus says to the company of his disciples: "Absolutely! And it is about this selfsame mission that *I will build my church* . . . and the gates of hell will not be able to prevail to keep it from happening."[2]

Think about it! Think what Jesus has just said. Think what it means. Think how it answers Alan's question to me. If Jesus' enigmatic affirmation—and his declaration of his intention to build the church—is followed by another enigmatic statement about the inevitable attempt by the gates of hell to destroy it . . . shouldn't that, then, be some kind of a major warning signal put there, on our trail, to warn us of a persistent and continual hazard? Like, if Jesus' affirmation is any indication of the certainty of God-in-Christ rescuing this lost creation, and calling out the community that will be his agent in accomplishing such a mission, notwithstanding the hellish opposition . . . then doesn't that indicate to us that, if I may express it this way, the forces of *hell* are sure as *hell* to try like *hell* to prevail and to stop Christ's building of his church, with all malicious intention and by every devious device in Satan's infernal arsenal?

The whole of the New Testament is a testimony to this cosmic conflict between Jesus' messianic mission to create all things new, and the satanic counter-effort to keep it from ever happening. It may be most clearly focused in a brief and awesome statement by the Apostle John: "The reason the Son of God appeared was to destroy the works of the devil."[3] Upon reflection, we see a concerted, diabolical attempt to keep Jesus, the Christ, from his mission from the very beginning. Think of Herod's *massacre of the innocents*, after Jesus' birth, when he learned that this child might be the long-awaited Messiah who would occupy David's throne—and so threaten his own throne.

Think of Jesus' encounter with Satan immediately after his baptism at the Jordan River by John. If you think about it, it is a weird account—like Satan just poised and waiting to deflect Jesus from his God-given mission. It's like Satan saying to Jesus, "Hey! I know who you are, and know why you have come, and what you are to do . . . and have I got a good deal for you! I've got a wonderful alternative plan that will be much easier and much less painful to you. Do you know that I can give you the kingdoms of the world without a cross? All you have to do is just bow down and worship me, become part of my dominion. Or, you could turn

2. My paraphrase of Matt 16:18.
3. 1 John 3:8.

these stones into bread and become an economic power and acquire popular acclaim by feeding the hungry. Or maybe attain popular power by leaping off of the temple and watching God's angels rescue you. The crowds will love it, and will follow you. Sound good?"

Satan, right there at the very threshold, sensed why Jesus had come. From that point, he set about to subvert the mission. Satan saw why Jesus had come and immediately sought to enlist him in his cosmic rebellion. Jesus saw right through that diabolical scheme. He knew from all eternity why he had to come, and that his mission required the cross. He would not be deflected, and, so, bluntly rebuked Satan's attempted subversion.

Think of Jesus, then, moving into the Palestinian scene, heralding the good news of the Kingdom of God, and in demonstration of the God-given authority of that Kingdom casting out demons, healing the sick, cleansing the lepers, and raising the dead, all in a fulfillment of prophecies about the signs that would accompany the coming of the messiah, signs which were given centuries before through the writings of the Hebrew prophets.

Throughout Jesus' earthly ministry, there were those moments when Jesus sensed Satan's attempts to thwart God's plan of salvation, for which he had come. When Satan could not accomplish his malicious subversion through other seductions, he determined that his only recourse then was to destroy Jesus. Satan could never have conceived that by that very act of seeking to destroy Jesus God's purpose would be accomplished. It was through the cross that he himself (Satan) would be disarmed and dethroned . . . and, in principle, destroyed.

It is in the context of all of that conflict with the prince of darkness that Jesus' words to his disciples at Caesarea Philippi—about "the gates of hell" seeking to destroy the church—begins to make sense.

Or stop and think, for a moment, about the commission that this same ascended Christ gave to Paul—apostle, missionary, church planter—as his missionary mandate: "Go and turn men and women from darkness to light, and from the power of Satan to God."[4] That very mandate later became a vital part of Paul's testimony before King Agrippa. Register that mandate carefully in its entirety. Subsequently, Paul will remind the believers at Colossae that God has delivered them from the *dominion* of darkness and has transferred them into the *Kingdom* of his

---

4. Acts 26:18.

beloved son.[5] Out of one dominion and into another—got it? Two dominions: Satan's and God's. So why are we surprised when the church continually gets led astray, or subverted, or confused about its design and purpose?

The context of our journey is not neutral.

Or maybe... remember that the Lord's Prayer is bracketed between a petition, at the beginning, for the Father's Kingdom to be coming, and his will to be done on earth,... and a petition, at the end, that we might be delivered from the *evil one*.[6] And, if those are not sufficient, think of Paul giving a sober warning to the Christians in Asia Minor that the real battle in which they were engaged was not with merely human adversaries, but with the wiles of the devil, with *principalities and powers*, with spiritual hosts of wickedness, and with all kinds of ominous supernatural entities.[7]

If that were still not enough to wake us up, then the whole wonderful book of Revelation is an eloquent pastoral study on this cosmic battle between the beast and the Lamb. That final book of the New Testament is given, out of the heart of God, to enable the church to know of the cosmic battle raging within the church's existential struggles in this age.

Hello!

THE COSMIC LANDSCAPE

All of that should begin to indicate to us something of the cosmic landscape in which we make our journey here, or the larger context into which our trail takes us. What is obvious is a kind of a biblical *cosmology* that involves two dominions that exist inimical to one another, and with no neutral territory in between.

That being so, when we have asked the questions: What is the church called out *of*? And then, conversely, What is the church called *into*?... the answer should begin to emerge, shouldn't it? There is, on one hand, God's creation now in cosmic rebellion against its Creator and inhabited by the *god of this world*. The Apostle John will say quite plainly that the whole world lies in the power of the evil one.[8] Paul will say of

---

5. Col 1:13.
6. Matt 6:9–13.
7. Eph 6:10–12.
8. 1 John 5:19.

those who have not responded to the message of Christ that "the god of this world has blinded the minds of the unbelievers, to keep them from seeing the light of the gospel of the glory of Christ."[9]

On the other hand is God's great and ultimate plan—his eschatological design—to reconcile the world to himself through the cross of Christ, and to create all things new, and to make the church integral to this design as it becomes the Body of Christ in the world, and the "missionary arm of the Trinity."[10]

Let me come back to the word *cosmology*.[11] This is not at all a minor point, as we are pursuing the question, What is the church? It may be useful to quote here from the biblical scholar Gregory Boyd:

> . . . *Jesus and his earliest disciples believed that the universe was inhabited by a myriad of spiritual beings, some good and some evil, which were at war with one another. And they believed that Jesus was the decisive player in this warfare.*
>
> *The most fundamental unifying theme throughout Jesus' ministry is that he was setting up the Kingdom of God over against the kingdom of Satan. Jesus' exorcistic and healing ministry constitutes preliminary victories over this enemy, while his death and resurrection spell Satan's ultimate demise.*
>
> *Yet even Jesus' victory over death was eschatological. It pointed beyond itself into the future, a future in which his accomplishment would be manifested. Though Jesus' death in principle 'drove out' the cosmic murderer (John 12:31; 8:44), this victory has not yet been manifested in the world, for people continue to die. Though Satan's fortress has in principle been toppled and the strong man himself 'tied up,' his fortress has not yet been toppled to the ground. Though the power to set people free from the scourges of this enemy has in principle been established and distributed to all who follow Christ, the world continue to be held hostage by this (now mortally wounded and bound) strong man (1 John 5:19).*

---

9. 2 Cor 4:4.

10. I recall this usage from the writings of José Míguez of Buenos Aires, Argentina. I shall be using it along the way because I think it says something quite critical.

11. *Cosmology*: A branch of systematic philosophy that deals with the character of the universe as a cosmos by combining speculative metaphysics and scientific knowledge: esp. a branch of philosophy that deals with the processes of nature and the relationship of its parts—compare ontology. 2. A particular theory or body of doctrine relating to the natural order. Etc. (*Webster's Third New International Dictionary*).

> *As the New Testament authors realize, this means there is still work to be done, and the church is the means by which it is to be done. In the time between the 'already' of Christ's work and the 'not yet' of the eschaton, the church is to be about what Jesus was about. It is, in a real sense, his 'body' here on earth. As such, the church is to be an extension of the ministry he himself carried out in his incarnate body while here on earth (2 Cor 5:18-19).*[12]

There is, then, on one hand, God's good creation: that which reflects God's nature and purpose and glory: "The heavens declare the glory of God, and the firmament displays his handiwork."[13] Into that good creation was introduced a cosmic rebellion, with all kinds of dimensions of darkness, destruction, confusion, supernatural beings, rebellious angels, bondage, illness, and challenges, to the design and purpose and glory of God. Right at the dawn of God's good creation, then, came the satanic instigation that challenged God's integrity, authority, and goodness. Some conveniently refer to that tragic event as "the fall." Others refer to it as "the crime." This is the dominion of darkness.

Yet, this whole creation is God's. It is his glory. God has no intention of abandoning it to this arch-rebel angelic being who comes, early on the scene, in the form of a serpent. Immediately, after the fall, there comes the first hint of God's redemptive design, the promise of the "seed of the women" who would bruise the serpent's head.[14] From that amazing revelation of the cosmic conflict—in which we also now find ourselves—the biblical record is a missionary document through and through. It is about God's eschatological design to rescue his creation from Satan's blight and malice, and to destroy Satan's works.

It begins to take significant form in the scriptural accounts of God communicating with Abraham, indicating that in Abraham's seed all the ethnic groups (nations) of the world would be blessed. There follows, then, the calling of the children of Israel to be a nation of priests. Later is given the Davidic promise of a "forever throne." In Israel's later history, there will come the message of the Old Testament prophets reflecting upon God's missionary and redemptive intention through the coming of one anointed by God: a *messiah*. Concerning this *promised one*, there are

---

12. Gregory Boyd, *God At War* (Downers Grove: InterVarsity Press), pp. 238-39.
13. Ps. 19:1.
14. Gen 3:15.

made awesome prophecies about his God-anointed ministry to reconcile the world to God, and to make all things new: God's Messiah.

All of this unfolds into splendid revelation as Jesus, God's own son, comes into the human scene as the "Word made flesh." This *Word of God* becomes truly human in Jesus of Nazareth. Jesus comes onto the Palestinian scene announcing the joyous news of the inauguration of God's new creation: the Kingdom of God. Jesus comes onto the scene heralding the message that God's long-awaited reign is on the threshold. He demonstrates his Kingdom authority by challenging Satan's dominion with healings, exorcisms, and other miraculous signs. Jesus' context is, on one hand, *this present age.* On the other hand, there is his announcement of the eschatological *age to come*, which he is inaugurating—by his incarnation and especially by his cross. On the cross, Jesus will dethrone and disarm Satan, and, in principle, destroy Satan's works.

NO NEUTRAL TERRITORY FOR THE CHURCH

Let's "cut to the chase" here and establish that there is never, anywhere in scripture, any hint that the church is to be a calling-out into some nebulous religious never-never-land. There is certainly no indication of any in-between neutral territory. There is no bland religious safe-zone into which we may escape. And there is never any suggestion of some kind of inspirational religious society with aesthetic worship services that are oblivious to the praise of the Lamb of God and to the eschatological mission of God.[15] **The calling of Jesus is a calling to have a radical change of understanding and of ultimate loyalty. It is a calling out of an enslaving dominion of darkness, and a calling into the liberating Kingdom of God's dear son.**

The word the New Testament uses for that radical called-for change is the word *repent*. Those who hear the invitation of Christ are called upon to get the true picture of what is going on, both in their lives and in this cosmos in which we live. It is an invitation to believe in God's great search-and-rescue mission in Christ. A response of repentance and faith engages us right away in Jesus' primary work, which is "to destroy the

---

15. Wendell Berry has a delicious description of such churches: "so preoccupied incanting anemic souls into heaven" (In "Christianity and the Survival of Creation," in *Sex, Economy, Freedom and Community*, New York, Pantheon, 1993, p. 114).

works of the devil."[16] Jesus has come to disarm principalities and powers by his cross.[17]

That's a whole marvelous study in itself.[18] It is a calling, by the mercy and love of God, to renounce that life that is part of the rebellious dominion of darkness, and to come into that whole New Creation that is reconciled to God and demonstrates God's great love for his creation. It is a calling *out of the dominion of darkness* and a calling *into the Kingdom of God's dear son*. It is a calling to forsake a whole way of living and thinking that is part of Satan's darkness, and to embrace a whole new life in God. It is a calling out of the merely human and into the divinely inhabited design of God. This is what Jesus' promise is all about: "Peace I leave with you: my peace I give unto you."[19]

Ah! Now we're back to the church—back to the called-out assembly that Jesus announced he would build, when he introduced this concept to his disciples at Caesarea Philippi. Yes, and we're also back to Alan's question about how a church can get so far afield, so out-of-it, into such institutional expressions as those with which he is involved.

FILTERS, FORGETFULNESS, AND SUBVERSIONS

It only follows, then, that the prince of darkness, i.e., the gates of hell, will employ whatever means available or conceivable to neuter, or render ineffective, this called-out assembly of the Messiah's people. There will always be the subtle erosions and teleological forgetfulness that will reduce the church to a merely human, or humanly explainable, religious institution. Yes, and—please take note—there will always be some ambiguities, in this community that is always in process.

Our trail into refounding is not at all a new one, nor are the dangers associated with such a calling. Our becoming involved brings with it all of that which will attempt to hinder us from arriving at our goal. Such hazards are not at all unique to us. One has only to look at the New Testament documents to find that there is always, in them, the very insistent warning about the presence of satanic opposition. We would have to be blind not to see it.

16. 1 John 3:8.

17. Col 2:15.

18. I cannot commend too highly the two splendid studies by Gregory Boyd—*God at War* and *Satan and the Problem of Evil*—done by InterVarsity Press.

19. John 14:27.

As stated above, the final book of the Bible, Revelation, spells out this cosmic conflict between darkness and light in graphic imagery. It is a very necessary, artistic (replete with symbolism), and pastoral message that paints before us the ongoing battle between the beast and the Lamb. It begins with the awesome picture of the ascended Lord Jesus walking among the seven golden candlesticks—his church.

He instructs John to write to the seven churches in Asia Minor, which together compose for us something of an "every church"—even though they were real assemblies. They existed within a generation or two of their apostolic foundings. Already most of them, along with the good stuff they were doing, were beginning to wander off of the path of their calling. They were forgetting true priorities and first loves. They were absorbing alien teachings and ethical aberrations. There were within them some pathological personalities, not to mention preoccupations with their own comfortable inner life . . . all very familiar problems. (It's interesting that the couple of churches that were undergoing the most severe persecution seem to be the ones that remembered what they were!) The risen Lord calls upon those churches to get back on track, in so many words: "Repent. I know what you are going through and I am with you, but remember who you are and to what you are called." This is the basic message.

After that, John is taken up on into the heavens, and before him is unfolded a panorama of the warfare that is ongoing in this between-the-ages context of the church's journey. In a remarkable, almost (one could say) impressionistic set of pictures, we are shown the saints in heaven giving worship to God and the Lamb. We see a portrayal of a dragon seeking to destroy the child of a woman and the child being protected. Its effort having failed, the beast then seeks to destroy the church, and so, also, the church is being protected. We see saints struggling and praying and determining history. The saints overcome the devil by "the blood of the Lamb, the word of their testimony, and they love not their lives unto the death."[20]

But, in the finale, Satan's destruction—accomplished in principle at the cross—is ultimately consummated, and he and his legions are cast into the lake of fire. With cosmic rejoicing, the Lamb is enthroned. The great eschatological mission is fulfilled. The beautiful bride is perfected

---

20. Rev 12:11).

and presented to the Lamb. God dwells with his people, and the New Heaven and New Earth is complete, and God is all and in all.

Wow! Awesome.

But, then, we need to take note. Between now and then the church is continually engaged in that warfare portrayed in Revelation. The beast is doing everything in his power—culturally, economically, socially, politically, ecclesiastically, and in every other way—to keep that ultimate consummation from happening. This is no hidden or mysterious interpretation. Paul reminds the church consistently that our real battle is not with merely human forces, but with principalities and powers and rulers and cosmic authorities—maybe even ecclesiastical principalities and powers![21] He speaks of Satan masquerading inside the church in the form of "angels of light" and "servants of righteousness"[22]—yes, even using those who are believers in their unguarded lives.

In all of this, Paul points us to the reality of the church's authority in the battle: ". . . so that through the church the manifold wisdom of God might be made known to rulers and authorities in heavenly places."[23] The church's calling into Christ is to be engaged in his mission, in which he has, by the cross, disarmed the rulers and authorities and put them to open shame,[24] and so given to us—to the church—his authority in his ongoing warfare with the beast, until the consummation, when Satan's destruction is complete.

This is our trail, then, as it has been the trail for God's church over the centuries—from the very beginning.

There are frightening episodes of the political and cultural principalities making massive assaults on the church, seeking to destroy it, or to disenfranchise it, or to make it some kind of a pariah. That was certainly true early on in the Roman Empire. It is still often true in those regions where other religions are dominant, and seek exclusivity, and so outlaw the church. It was certainly true in the twentieth century when the Cultural Revolution in China sought to exterminate the

---

21. (Eph 6:12).

22. 2 Cor 11:12–15. That could conceivably be interpreted as pastors, teachers, and church leaders who are "ordained," and perhaps even believers, but who succumb again to the agenda of the dominion of darkness. Note, in this passage are false apostles and deceitful workmen masquerading . . .

23. Eph 3:10.

24. Col 2:15.

church. Interestingly, when the church has been frontally assaulted and persecuted, it has come out cleaner and bolder and stronger and more fruitful.

More often, the assaults of the principalities and powers and rulers—the gates of hell—of this age, seeking to prevail against the church, operate in less ominous, and much more subtle and even sophisticated ways: drift, forgetfulness, misplaced priorities, complacency, alien teachings embraced in some syncretistic way, compromise, peace made with the rulers and the dominant social order—all of which, at the time, seem harmless, but which erode and eviscerate the church's power and integrity. The temptation is to dilute the message so as to make it less offensive.[25]

All so seemingly innocent. The darkness begins to encroach again. It is all so real to one generation, and then time passes, and a new generation finds it all only an interesting custom or memory. And behind the scenes is the one who hates the Lamb and his church. Satan is clever and is too smart to be obvious: "angels of light," the wrong focus, distinguished members giving Satan place in their lives (like Ananias and Sapphira in the book of Acts) . . . the darkness seeps in, quietly, and the church's power and witness are diminished. What happens is that the church reverts to the merely human, i.e., to an assembly without the indwelling Spirit, and one that has no integrity of connection with the Kingdom of God.

Once that happens, the church is inhabited comfortably by *nominal Christians*—Christians in name only—or what I prefer to call *unconverted believers*. These are folk who are enthusiastic about the church institution, but have hardly a clue as to its place in the eschatological mission of God. They tend to have no dynamic sense of repentance and faith, and can be completely casual about any signs of authenticity as obedient followers of Jesus Christ.

One of the church's earliest preserved hymns warns us: *"Christian, dost thou see them, on the holy ground? How the hosts of darkness rage thy*

---

25. In my own career it was sobering to watch so much of the Christendom church's silence during the Civil Rights Movement, and during the Vietnam War—these being controversial within the society, notwithstanding the ethical mandates of the Kingdom of God. One could make a case that the Christendom church today doesn't want to challenge the excesses of a consumer culture, or an entertainment culture, or the gospel of the global economy, or the gospel of American military dominance in the world. Better to truncate or redefine the church's mission to fit "the empire."

steps around..."[26] Also, the baptismal formula in many churches included for centuries a *renunciation*, i.e., a renouncing of Satan's dominion and all that was destructive, dehumanizing, etc., along with an announcing of one's intent to become a faithful follower of Jesus Christ. That, at least, kept the warfare somewhat part of the church's consciousness. But even that, over time and with drift, can too easily become mindlessly liturgical and meaningless.

TWO CULTURAL AND VERY DEBILITATING SUBVERSIONS

We tend to look locally at the workings of the forces of the kingdom of darkness, in this cosmological battle in which the church is engaged—the battle between darkness and light. But there are, at times, those larger cultural events—which emerge gradually and almost unnoticed—that seem so universally accepted and sophisticated that they are easily overlooked. They can be discounted, all too mindlessly, as having nothing to do with the church. It is only after the fact, and in retrospect, that we realize how devastating they have been, though often unrecognized.

To return to our trail metaphor, there are at times those natural phenomena, such as darkness, or storms, or dense fogs, which so completely obliterate our vision that it becomes difficult to discern the path. We know the trail continues somewhere, yet it is obscured for us. We lose orientation. The prince of darkness, the god of this world, will use any device to misdirect the church's good intention to be faithful, while at the same time neutering the church's missionary confrontation with the world, so that it compromises its very *raison d'être* in the design of God to make all things new.

Two of these phenomena deserve our special note:

1. "Constantinianization" and the emergence of the Christendom church.

2. The so-called "Enlightenment."

Neither of these took place in a moment of time, but they can be pegged, historically, to general periods, and as due to specific historical and cultural circumstances. I only raise them, at this point in our journey, because they are far too much the Christendom subversions that

---

26. The hymn "Christian, Dost Thou See Them?" is ascribed to Andrew of Crete in the seventh century, but is not making it into many contemporary hymnbooks!

have given shape to the church for the past millennium and a half. It is not that these forms are, in themselves, evil—it is only that they have too often subverted the church from its missional priorities. Our role at the threshold of the twenty-first century, then, will be to acknowledge their reality, their subversive nature, and perhaps to "deconstruct" them, and to seek to find our way again through them, to our intended teleology and missional focus.

THE EMERGENCE OF THE "CHRISTENDOM CHURCH"

The first several centuries of the new Christian movement are a study in themselves, replete with unbelievable missionary fruitfulness, doctrinal debates, struggles with self-understanding, engagement with new cultures . . . but mostly in an alien context, and as a minority cult, and with frequent persecutions both locally and by the imperial principalities and powers. Add to this the fact that this period did, indeed, include internal debates and conflicts as part of the movement's growing pains. But the church, in this period, was essentially a movement motivated by a passion to see the gospel of the Kingdom of God reach into every nation. The church, through all of this, was essentially a mobile, flexible, versatile missional community, becoming incarnate in simple forms—and inventing itself as it went along.

The church did indeed grow, and soon reached into the far reaches of the Roman Empire, and beyond. There was no assured security. For the church to confess that Jesus was the only true Lord was, in fact, to challenge the patriotic mantra of the Roman Empire, in which Caesar was the undisputed lord. The blood of many martyrs was spilt continually over such treasonous confessions. Such a witness by the Christian movement cost many a life, but the cost was actually even anticipated by those being baptized into it.

To use a term borrowed from missiologist Lesslie Newbigin, the church was continually in a self-conscious "missionary confrontation" with the rulers and authorities—i.e., with the political, social, economic, and cultural context of the real world in which it lived and witnessed. The church was quite self-conscious about its divine teleology, provoked, among other things, by the fact that it had no security in its here-and-now existence. It does not take much imagination to realize that there would be, at the same time, within the church, a longing for more stability, peace, and security, in its life, at some point. Yet, while it was living in the midst of this missionary movement, with all of its inherent dangers, the church grew exponentially until, by the third and fourth centuries, it was one of the most formidable communities in the deteriorating Roman Empire.

And so it was that in the early fourth century the Roman emperor Constantine professed to have seen a vision of the cross of Christ, and so he professed to having been converted to Christianity, for whatever reasons. It could have been a purely political move on his part, but it had immediate consequences for the church. The church, rather suddenly, and for the first time, became legitimized—it was no longer an outlaw or illegal religion. Constantine not only legitimized it, but he began to conform it to the patterns of the pagan religions of the empire. He bestowed on it all kinds of "perks." It was his intent that this newly confessed faith of his would have status in the empire. He did this by building for it sanctuaries, or temples. He encouraged the development of a class of priests, which included vestments and choirs in accord with all of the accoutrements that pagan religions had.

In so doing, he would conform the Christian church to the cultural expectations for a *true* religion. Constantine, by the way, also intruded himself into the church affairs by encouraging some of the ecumenical gatherings to resolve internal disputes. In essence, Constantine *co-opted* the church for the benefit of the empire.

All of that subtle and understandable subversion falls under the rubric of the Constantinianization of the church.

In the sixth century, the emperor Justinian took it all one step further and made Christianity the official religion of the empire. In so doing, he *established* the church, so that church and empire were indelibly linked and identified. To be baptized into the church was to become an official part of the empire, and vice-versa. The church was given status and was protected by the Roman government. The church became the chaplain to the empire, and the empire became the church's protector. Note the placement, ultimately, of the Vatican in the midst of the Imperial City of Rome. When the Roman armies went into pagan Europe, they required that conquered tribes be baptized or killed. (Is that a weird kind of evangelism, or what?)

What emerges is the Christendom church. By the tenth century, it was totally in place, and its whole life, liturgies, hierarchical structures, traditions, and ecclesial patterns were pretty much established.

As the Roman Empire declined, the Christendom church, in turn, grew in influence, and began to exercise control over the governments of the western world. We see it in such teachings as "the divine right of kings," and the affinity between church and state. We see it in the accounts of the church blessing the crusades in the Middle Ages. Even after the Reformation, nation-states traditionally had an official state church in most of Europe (the church in the East is a whole different study). This affinity comes right into the twenty-first century in the United States with the whole "Bible and flag" syndrome, or the "God bless America" mantras that politicians usually invoke at the end of speeches. We see it in the church's tax deductibility on property and finances. We also see it in court cases where the nation-state wants to tell churches what is proper to preach, and who should be able to be members.

The Christendom church, then, made peace with the empire. To put it more baldly, the church was thereby co-opted by—and all too much conformed to—the dominant social order. It thereby lost its counter-cultural essence and its freedom to be in missionary confrontation with the structures of the dominion of darkness. It became inappropriate for the church to do or say anything that would embarrass or rebuke the empire—or anything that reflected negatively on the empire—be it the political, economic, social, or even ecclesiastical expressions of the empire.[27] The church became the chaplain to the empire, which in return promised to protect the church. But there was a critical and costly compromise. Too often the Christendom church has become conformed to the darkness, and become a defender of the principalities and powers, which in turn of course neuters its faithfulness and power.

Is that radical? Of course it's radical! The church is to be a witness to the light of the Kingdom of God, and by virtue of that witness is often subversive of the political and cultural expressions of the dominion of darkness . . . "that through the church the manifold wisdom of God might be made to rulers and authorities in heavenly places." [28]

---

27. When one is seeking to define the principalities and powers that we confront, it is necessary to include the ecclesiastical principalities and powers as a subtle power that can also subvert true kingdom of God integrity.

28. Eph 3:10.

CLERGY

Another piece of the Christendom church, which came about generally with the same Constantinianization subversion, was the emergence of a priestly order within the church, which we designate as *clergy*. With such a category as clergy, you came to have a two-layered church: an active clergy, and a more passive laity. Sounds innocent enough to those of us who have come to accept these categories uncritically. The clergy were the official and ordained holy men (maybe a few women). They were the active part of the church. The church was, for all practical purposes, defined by the clergy. Then there were the laity, who were mostly passive and expected to be subservient to the clergy. The laity ultimately were not encouraged to see themselves as the dynamic cutting edge of the church's mission in their daily lives.

A significant dimension of this subversion has to do with the New Testament role of the *teaching shepherd*, or pastor-teacher, in the church's divine purpose. This gift was subverted, and re-defined, from being that of equipping the laity for their ministry, into something quite different. It became primarily a custodial role, called "pastoral care," in which the clergy performed the rites of the church, in which the laity could engage somewhat passively. (In a later trail guide, we will explore how the Spirit equips the church for its work.)

So, then emerged a church dominated by a sacralized class of clergy. Alas!

When you add to that bit of subversion, so understandable, the focus that the Christendom church began to put on church buildings—which are never a part of the New Testament community—you get another major distraction from the missionary movement. The church with its *sanctuaries*, or its sacralized buildings, became a *rooted* church. With its focus on the place rather than the mission, the church became *grounded* rather than being versatile and mobile. The church gathered in a sacred place. How often the church building, its sanctuary, has become an idol to the gathered congregation. That *place*, rather than the missional community, became the church. The sanctuary rather than the real world was where one found God. Sound familiar?

To summarize, then, you have coming, almost clandestinely, into the church's acceptance, two pieces of its self-understanding that totally redefined the church into something that Jesus had never taught nor intended. There is nowhere in the New Testament any indication that the church was to build sanctuaries, or that it was to declare some buildings "sacralized." Quite the opposite. The church was a missionary movement, not rooted in buildings. The temple of God, in the New Testament, is found in the lives and community of Christ's followers. And there is no sacralized class of priests, no clergy. The church was something of an egalitarian community in which the ascended Lord Jesus gave gifts to *all* of its adherents, and one of those gifts was to equip all of God's people for their mature participation in the church's mission. (That's for a later Trail Guide!)

No sacralized buildings, and no sacralized class of clergy: these are inimical to the missional design of Jesus for his church. Yet the subversion of this has been all too much its self-understanding now for a millennium and a half.

Let me hasten to assure the readers of this trail guide that this is not to say that God abandoned the church at all. Expressions of missional obedience and Kingdom consciousness emerge with regularity. Jesus is irresistibly building his church. At the same time the gates of hell are not passive. This *is* to say, however, that the church in its Christendom expression basically became humanly explainable, and much less than that demonstration of the Holy Spirit and power that it was intended to communally incarnate in the world.

Nor do I intend to imply that a church institution—in distinction from a Christendom church institution—may not be a powerful staging area for the church's mission. When the Word of Christ dwells richly among God's people, and when the church community embraces passionately the mission of God in Christ . . . then that church institution and its rites and its professional staff can be a significant factor in realizing the church's teleology. But such healthy institutions must be continually on guard against being co-opted by strong Christendom subversion, which can be so conducive to nominal Christianity. Such consciousness-raising about this danger is one significant part of the underside church's role.

That's major cultural subversion Number One.

THE ENLIGHTENMENT
(CIRCA: THE SEVENTEENTH CENTURY)

There is still another major and subtle cultural subversion whose influence permeates our ecclesiastical atmosphere.

There were all of those centuries in which the Church of Rome completely dominated the culture in the western world. The church owned the universities, trained their faculties, intimidated kings and rulers, and determined much of what was acceptable to believe and do—and redefined *the church* to reinforce its dominance.

Yet, there were always present those underside communities, and those restless followers of Jesus, who, along with many more secular persons of influence and intelligence, questioned and challenged and preserved their integrity. This is illustrated, in many instances, by the emergence of the Roman Catholic orders, which orders were frequently underside communities. There were undoubtedly numerous unrecognized cohorts of believers, meeting, praying, discussing, remembering Christ's teachings.[29]

It was in the late middle ages that there emerged a major cultural-intellectual movement called the *Renaissance*. The Renaissance became a formative factor as the academic-intellectual world began to break out of its ecclesiastical captivity and to think afresh, to explore, to investigate, and to challenge previous assumptions. That Renaissance had its effect, as well, in the ecclesiastical world. One could make the case that the Protestant Reformation of the sixteenth century had roots deeply in that Renaissance movement.

But even as the church and the academy were liberated from the controlling influence of Rome and the Vatican, there emerged still another cultural and intellectual movement, which we call the *Enlightenment*. This movement was of enormous—actually incalculable—influence. Out of its intellectual energy came the political philosophy of John Locke, the scientific method of Francis Bacon and Isaac Newton, and the rationalistic principles of such a giant figure as Rene Descartes. Lots of good stuff here. It permeates the culture of the academy to this day, in spades. It is responsible for the whole era that we now designate the *Modern Era*.

But, note how the church bought into this Enlightenment movement, to its enrichment, but also to its detriment, as many of the movement's positions were inimical to the church essence as the dwelling place of God by the Spirit. We're not talking here about some crude and obvious, frontal satanic assault on the church. We're suggesting,

---

29. One thinks of the Waldensians and the undoubted presence of many others throughout this period.

rather, a very subtle and sophisticated sowing of a virus, which *de-supernaturalized* the Christian faith and Christian church. It, in essence, reduced the church to something merely human, or humanly explainable, and rendered it much less than the supernatural dwelling place of God by the Holy Spirit. Faith and spirituality became private affairs, but with no recognized status in the public square. Faith may be good for a person in private, but faith and theology and their claims could not, by Enlightenment standards, stand the scrutiny of rationalism and the scientific method, which came to dominate the culture.

Even though many of the major figures in the Enlightenment were part of the church, there was, at the same time, an underlying assumption that the church was a merely human religious institution and, thereby, could be explained by human reason, and formed by merely human political principles. Cartesian rationalism showed up as the church began to define its leadership all too much in terms of academic credentials, intellectual acumen, and theological expertise—as valuable as these might be—rather than by the Spirit-inhabited lives and communities it led, or its proven gifts. The Christian community was an acceptable religious institution and a symbol of stability in society . . . so long as it knew its place. But it was no longer generally expected to be the demonstration of a fruitful, New Creation community, living in missionary confrontation with the cultural expressions of the dominion of darkness. One could say that the church's counter-cultural, Kingdom of God essence was replaced by merely human standards congenial to the dominant social order.

Who notices? To be qualified to be ordained as a church leader now often requires a Master of Divinity degree, the requirements of which degree are defined by secular accrediting agencies. Oh!

Or, in biblical studies, all that is overtly supernatural in scriptures, and that cannot be explained by the scientific method, becomes suspect. This is devastating to the dynamic of inspiration, of prophecy, of the divine-human nature of Christ, of the resurrection, of the gifts of the Holy Spirit, of miracles, of divine revelation, of conversion . . . or anything that is beyond a merely human religious explanation. All this notwithstanding that the apostle warns us that " . . . not many of you were wise according to worldly standards, not many were powerful, not many were of noble birth. But God chose what is foolish in the world to shame the wise; God chose what is weak in the world to shame the strong; God chose what is low and despised in the world, even things that are not, to bring to nothing things that are, so that no human being might boast in the presence of God."[30]

A sizeable part of the western church establishment will bristle with defensiveness at such a statement. Again, this is not, in any way, to denigrate human skills and intelligence . . . except as God's Kingdom people are taken captive, in their behavior and thinking, by a subversive worldview that cannot even see the Kingdom of God. The gospel of the Kingdom of God is quite radical and explainable only in a worldview that far transcends the merely human.

FORGETFULNESS AND ITS ACCOMPANYING DRIFT BACK INTO THE DARKNESS

This is, perhaps, the most pernicious of the subversions that explain, in answer to my friend Alan's initial question of me, how the church gets so out-of-it.

A number of years ago, there was a humorous cartoon in the *New Yorker* that portrayed the runner Pheidippides—who had run the 25 miles from Marathon to Athens to tell the elders of the military victory that had been won against the Persians—standing there, dumbfounded before the elders, with this bewildered look on his face, and confessing, "I forgot the message."

That cartoon may elicit some good laughs, but, unfortunately, the church easily and continually forgets its message, its *raison d'être*, its identity with the mission of God in Jesus Christ . . . and reverts to a comfortable religious institution with many entertaining activities, but which is essentially *gospel-less*. For the first generation of those who have had a dynamic encounter with Jesus Christ, it is all so compelling and alive with the reality of their calling, and with the transformed lives given them by the Holy Spirit. They write hymns. They cause the Word of Christ to dwell richly among themselves. They engage in mutual ministries of building each other up in faith and obedience. They are contagious with the gospel, engaged in Christ's mission, and producing the fruits of the Spirit.

Then, there comes the second generation, for which it is all a bit more removed, and that initial experience may be a bit more of a memory, still influential but second-hand. There tends to be an almost indis-

---

30. 1 Cor 1:26–29.

cernible drift back toward the thinking and behavior of the darkness. But the community of faith is still important somehow. But, then . . . the third generation passes, and the years go by . . . and it all becomes a story from the past, barely a memory, and not at all a formative reality. The writer of the Letter to the Hebrews states it this way: "Therefore we must pay much closer attention to what we have heard, lest we *drift* from it."[31]

Gerald Arbuckle, Roman Catholic priest and cultural anthropologist, did a seminal study of how and why his own Maryknoll Order was diminishing in size and influence, which study relates very powerfully to answering Alan's question of me.[32] Arbuckle's conclusion is that any "order" (translate that to *Christian community*, or *church*) is founded or formed out of "chaos" by what he terms a "founding myth." So long as that founding myth is dynamic in its life and thinking, the order is vital and fruitful. But, he concludes (in so many words) that whenever that founding myth is "diluted, displaced, or forgotten," then the order reverts to chaos.

So it is with the church. So long as its calling, out of the dominion of darkness and into the Kingdom of God's dear son, is dynamic in its midst, so long as its divine teleology[33] forms the consciousness of the community, then that church is vital. But once that sense of calling is *diluted*, *displaced*, or *forgotten*, then the church reverts to the thinking and behavior of the kingdom of darkness—to chaos.

Through these subversions, the church becomes captive to the culture and forgetful of its eschatological calling, rather than remaining a transformational force within the lives of its adherents and within the culture. We, in the church, become merely human religious folk, determining our course by human philosophies, and by human therapies, rather than by demonstration of the Holy Spirit and power—and, even though we may mouth the gospel's words in our gatherings, we tend to do so rather mindlessly.

---

31. Heb 2:1.

32. See Arbuckle, *Out of Chaos* and *Refounding the Church*.

33. I am constrained also to remind my readers that the divine power that accompanies that teleology is very much a *sine quo non* in the formation of the new creation community.

The gates of hell prevail within all too much of our traditional church scene.

But Jesus continues to build his church, and to break in and break out, when least expected, in order to rescue his lost creation. Our task as the underside church is to insist upon a clear vision, and a clear sense, of our identity with Jesus and the mission of God, so that we will know how to be a refounding influence that will encourage the church back into the church's God-given teleology—to be formed by the Word of Christ and the dynamic presence of the Holy Spirit.

There is a malignant counter-force, subtle and sophisticated, that energizes this drift and forgetfulness within the church—along with all the other subversions—to keep the church from its calling . . . and it has a personality and a name. It is called Satan, a.k.a. the gates of hell. "Deliver us from the evil one."

> *"Christian, seek not yet repose,"*
> *Hear thy guardian angel say;*
> *Thou are in the midst of foes;*
> *Watch and pray.*
>
> *Principalities and powers,*
> *Mustering their unseen array,*
> *Wait for thy unguarded house;*
> *Watch and pray.*
>
> —Charlotte Elliott, 1839

SPECIFICS FOR THE TRAIL

Given our agreed upon mission—that of refounding the church from the underside—we are always keenly aware that the ecclesiastical culture we inhabit as the underside is probably, and primarily, formed by the Christendom mentality. It becomes a delicate role, then, and a role that requires much wisdom and humility, to know how to encourage our pockets of leaven and light amid such forgetful and distracted church expressions. How to do this, while, at the same time, affirming those dimensions that are profitable and harmonious with the gospel of the

Kingdom, and how to carry out such a ministry with joy and thanksgiving, will keep us on our toes.

It may be enough to simply engage in continual consciousness-raising and mutual encouragement with each other in our refounding colonies, and to maintain a generous willingness to be agents of God's love and gospel . . . while at the same time reserving our need, at times, to quietly resist—to live counter-culturally (kingdomly) within the Christendom subversion—without becoming captive to the Christendom mentality. Add to that the need of a continual prayer for discernment! It is never simple to both *protest* and *affirm* in love. Our Kingdom authenticity begins with us, and then with our underside companions. Our covenant with each other will be to attempt by the Spirit to demonstrate the authenticity of the New Creation community.

Such an underside community is most often lived in churches whose leadership is essentially formed by the Christendom mentality, which leadership is seeking to faithfully carry out the role assigned to it by that (subverted) definition of the church that is at odds with our understanding of the church's Kingdom teleology. Such requires much sensitivity, humility, and patience on our part. It may be primarily a ministry of prayer for the refounding of understanding and structure of this same scene.

Trail Guide #3

Refounding the Church from the Underside

It is necessary here to point out to my fellow exiles within the church, whatever the particular ecclesiastical setting for their sojourn might be—which setting can frequently be forgetful and unfaithful—that in a very real sense Christ's church is always out of control . . . just as the gospel is always out of control! Why is this so? It is so simply because it is Jesus Christ himself who is building his church. After all, the church is his divine intent and his creation—not ours. It is Jesus Christ, then, who is sovereignly working from within his people to fulfill the promise, given to Abraham, that in Abraham's seed should all the nations be blessed. Jesus is that seed.

It is absolutely going to happen!

When its human components become forgetful of their calling or of their authenticity as the people of God's New Creation in Christ—and become idolatrous about their institutions and sanctuaries—then, count on it . . . Jesus will do some creative "end-run," raise up a movement, call forth some faithful folk and anoint them with his Spirit, cause the gospel of the Kingdom to permeate a society like leaven . . . or do something where no one is looking, and the progress assuredly will go on until every knee bows and every tongue confesses that Jesus Christ is Lord. It is Jesus Christ who builds his church.

That point made, then, we are back to our own incarnation in our very real, *here and now*, traditional Christendom churches.

Let me, then, remind you that the New Testament doesn't really give us many clues as to the *form* of the church. Okay?[1] The church in those first couple of generations had to have been basically growing and mul-

---

1. N.T. Wright notes (somewhere) in *Jesus And The People Of God* that the church really did not have any unified and mutually held ecclesiastical form . . . even in the earliest days. It seems to have invented itself as it spread.

tiplying in very small communities (undoubtedly in some communication with each other), and in a variety of informal and non-institutional settings. How it grew, from a few thousand to perhaps twenty million, in a couple of centuries, to near-dominate the Roman Empire, is a marvel and something of a mystery, simply because the records are so sparse.

Early on the *people of the Way*, the followers of Jesus, seem to have found Jewish synagogues as a common place of contact in their initial missional outreach, since most of the believers in Jerusalem were of Jewish roots. Such synagogues were pretty much present in all the urban centers across the Roman world because of the Jewish dispersion. These tended to be, at least, the missionary Paul's initial points of contact. These new followers of Christ met, however, in many venues. We know that homes were a primary meeting place. Then, Paul met others by the riverside in Philippi, or in a rented meeting hall in Corinth.

Perhaps one of the most enlightening models for us—and perhaps giving some insight into the growth of the first century church—is what has happened in China in the decades since 1948, at the time of the Communist takeover, and more intensely later in the Cultural Revolution. At that time, the Christian church in China could be inventoried at some . . . what? Eight million? Now, these decades later, it is estimated at somewhere between eighty and one hundred million. How did that happen?

Answer: *the church out of control.*

When the church was dispossessed of its buildings and physical assets, its human confidences, and was outlawed . . . what did it do? It essentially went underground into clandestine conventicles, into house churches and secret gatherings.

There was, to be sure, the government approved and controlled church, known as the Three-Self Church, but it was more powerless and somewhat compromised. However it took place, the clandestine and underground church was without formal structure, but with vigorous networks and equipping principles (as per Ephesians 4) that permeated the vast Chinese nation. Accounts have reported that when some of those Chinese followers of Christ were arrested and put into concentration camps for professing Christ, they then no longer had to be secretive, and so became bold heralds of the gospel of the Kingdom in those very concentration camps. The out of control church made concentration camps to be mother lodes of gospel outreach! Fascinating.

Now, to our reality check.

Our own existential context is not in those first two centuries, nor is it in China in the twentieth . . . but, most frequently, it is a context of what some have designated "the *churchy churches* of a Christendom variety." These are very common in our very real, present, post-Christian, western world of the twenty-first century. Our sojourn is in the established and acceptable and comfortable and traditional church institutions with little vision of life beyond their own spiritual comfort-zone, with a modest record of good works or institutional success, and of modest reputation. They usually have western culture written all over them. Am I right?

But . . . over all of these intervening centuries, and in subverted churches, which have accommodated their institutional lives to the dominant social order . . . in congregations impressive for their buildings and liturgies and clergy and stained glass windows and marvelous choirs and hymnology, in moribund congregations of many descriptions . . . something has been smoldering. Such ecclesial scenes may have been, to all outward appearances, spiritually powerless and non-expectant, and certainly without any Kingdom or missional priorities . . . yet they were frequently the surprising context in which there were those clandestine underside churches, which resisted the dominant context and expressed salt and light—and incarnated the gospel.

Yet, in such scenes there have, very frequently, been those *exiles*, such as you and I, who have longed, and prayed, and equipped each other—who have met in homes, or around tables, or at picnics, or in pubs—and sought to be faithful to Christ's commission, within these very same church expressions, even through many discouragements . . .

It is such small fellowships of exiles that make up what I am calling here *churches from the underside*. These are those modest companies of faithful, self-effacing saints who reflect the strength and sweetness of Christ to all with whom they come in contact. These are those who have a wholesome sense of what the church's eschatological and missional calling is all about.

These are the authentic communities that incarnate the gospel. These exiles, frequently without power, portfolio, or ecclesiastical recognition, are the dwelling place of God by the Holy Spirit. In these quiet and hidden underside communities dwell folk of faith in Jesus Christ, in lives of obedience formed in adoration. These are folk of humility and with gentle servant-spirits, who are content being out of sight—and yet the aroma of God is upon them. Hidden but powerful, these are, in many different forms and in innumerable people groups across the world, the underside church. These are the church out of control!

REFOUNDING?

That word *refounding*, that I have tossed into this discussion, deserves some definition. I like that word. I have already referred to the provocative writer, the Maryknoll father Gerald Arbuckle, who introduced me to this word, which speaks of those churches (or any Christian movement), which so often dilute, displace, or forget what he calls their "founding myth" (which is the term he uses to designate their reason for existence).

When this takes place, the church then loses its authenticity and power.[2] What such churches and Christian orders need, this author will propose, is much more than anything like a "revival" or a "renewal." What is required is something much more profound and radical. What is required, Arbuckle insists, is a *refounding*. What they need is to deliberately go back and build again on their true foundations, their true founding myth, and that refounding must be from the ground up. My thesis here is that this has to happen over and over again . . . and, so frequently in history, it has happened either obviously, or partially, or clandestinely, with and by the agency of the church from the underside.

Refounding seldom comes from the top down. It almost never comes from church councils, hardly ever from the ecclesiastical authorities. (Awakenings seldom begin in church committees!) These all—including a distressing number of so-called "church professionals"—are quite too much committed, too invested, and too captive to the Christendom institutional pattern, which empowers them.[3] Such underside churches happen, by the working of the Spirit of God, in gatherings of folk who are formed by the Word of Christ, and seek, in obedience, to be and do what Christ has mandated them to be and do.

---

2. See Arbuckle, *Refounding The Church*. Arbuckle is not talking about the founding myth as some fantasy or fiction, but rather that body of values, purposes, and beliefs that initiated the whole movement, order, or church in the first place.

3. And, one needs to note from unhappy experience, that such clergy wedded to the Christendom institution are frequently quite paranoid about anything that challenges their ecclesial assumptions!

Risky?

Of course it's risky! The church is always risky. It was risky for Jesus to ascend back to the Father and to leave the mission of God in the hands of such "weak reeds" as the twelve, but remember that he had taught them in the plainest terms that they could not ever depend upon their merely human resources: "It is to your advantage that I go away, for if I do not go away the Helper will not come to you."[4]

Risk, then, is not really a concern, though many ecclesiastical authorities will blanch at the very idea of anything in the church happening without their sponsorship, or under their control. And that is simply the genius of Christ building his church, his missional communities of the Kingdom of God. It is by the dynamic of the Spirit at work in human lives and relationships that these spread like leaven in a loaf. (See Christ's own metaphor.)

Such pockets of life, such pods of faithful disciples, these powerful but out-of-sight gatherings of Christ's followers in church history are the strategic underside church. There is no rulebook for such. They are the product of the Spirit of God working in the people of God to incarnate the gospel of the Kingdom in their New Creation lives, and in their fellowship. Their prayers are that they may also edify, or build up and encourage those others with whom they frequently dwell within the church institutions. Such are true communal expressions of faith, hope, and love. They exist strategically out-of-sight, and, not infrequently, in the context of churchy churches that are missing the point. They are agents of grassroots refounding. There is an incarnational New Creation aroma and authenticity to their lives together, which expresses the fruits of the Spirit. That's my thesis.

A word of caution is in order. Where there is spiritual darkness, there is also quite evidently the presence of the prince of darkness. This means that these underside gatherings are also engaged in a strategic spiritual warfare. They may have prophetic eyes to see how the larger church has diluted, displaced, or forgotten its *raison d´être*, but their very presence within that larger scene is in reality a clash of dominions, and has its hazards, as many of us can testify.

One comes back, again and again, to Jesus' word to us that our calling is to *abide* in him, and for his word to abide in us. This means that we are to be the practitioners of a New Creation relationship in Christ,

---

4. John 16:7, in the context of Jesus' whole discourse recorded in John 14–16.

and through Christ, with the Triune God. Such quiet and gentle abiding also makes us vessels of the Holy Spirit and of true power. It makes of us those through whom the "streams of living water" may flow into the parched spiritual and ecclesial landscape around us.

I come back again to the example of Frodo in J. R. R. Tolkien's *The Lord of the Rings* trilogy (referred to in Trail Guide # 1). The hobbit Frodo knew that his calling and sojourn was fraught with danger, but that its successful conclusion would bring renewed hope and life and joy to Middle Earth, and especially to the Shire, which was his home. His task was to keep out of sight, and to quietly and secretly find his way to Mt. Doom, and to destroy the Ring of Power. All around him during those long days and weeks were the malicious and infernal agents of the dark lord. So Frodo—and his faithful companion Sam—kept a low profile. So it is with our underside churches. We may quite deliberately engage in our journey of faithful discipleship with a low profile, yet our redemptive purpose is that of ultimately bringing a presence of true gospel—streams of living water—into the socio-economic-ecclesiastical context of our lives.

Such underside churches are free to ask questions, to be honest, to explore, and to pray about intractable involvements. There are, to be sure, inescapable questions that need to be asked about many ecclesiastical institutions, which questions are not ultimately impertinent, or cynical, or inappropriate when discussed with each other. Questions such as: Maybe ours is not even a church—but then it's all that we've got!—what do we do? Is it conceivable that a significant portion of the church (and especially the Christendom church, or the churchy church) doesn't even know what the gospel *is* in its larger eschatological and biblically dominant (gospel of the Kingdom) definition? Or, is it conceivable that much that passes for worship . . . *isn't* worship at all?

What, then, are we exiles (there are a lot of us) to do? These questions are for starts, but such questions must always be accompanied with lives of wisdom, humility, love, and knowledge.

SPECIFICS FOR THE TRAIL

There is a delicate and demanding discipline required from our underside church as it inhabits larger church institutions, which can, at times, seem so oblivious and resistant to any serious encounter with their calling and mission . . . their *teleology*. It is so easy to become restless at the wasted potential. So, at this point, we need to remember that, when Paul addressed the potentially divisive issue of the gifts of the Spirit in 1 Corinthians 12–14, he repeatedly came back to the core issue that the purpose of the gifts was for the building up (edification) of the church. That is our principle also. Our very existence as a refounding community demands that we keep in mind that our calling is not as critics, not as those who are negative, dyspeptic, pessimistic, or destructive, but as those who are to be positively, redemptively, joyfully, and lovingly building up the church.

Add to that the principle from 1 Corinthians—Paul's word to the brewing strife in Philippi—that we are to have in us the mind of Christ, who, though he was God, did not consider equality with God a thing to be grasped to himself, but who humbled himself and made himself of no reputation, and so became obedient to his calling to endure the cross. We, as the underside church, at all costs must seek that self-understanding. We are to be that servant people, self-effacing, being the "sweet savor of Christ" in our off-stage role as those whose calling is to build up the church. Yes, there are often those hungry sheep who look up and are not fed by those pertaining to be the pastors, but ours is not to succumb to the fruitless role of resident critics, but rather to gently become a leavening and redemptive influence in the midst of the forgetfulness, and the often ecclesiastical unfaithfulness of our own "You Are Here" incarnation.

Maybe a phrase borrowed from Henri Nouwen is in order here: "*Seek littleness!*"

Trail Guide # 4

Participation, Form, and Character of the Underside Community

WHAT I AM PROPOSING as the underside church is a small—clandestine, even—*leavening community*, which may dwell within any one of those multitudes of amnesiac Christendom institutions.[1] This makes it incumbent upon our underside church, then, that it be very self-conscious of its purpose: a) to be a microcosm of the re-creation of the human community as God intended the human community to be, and within the Trinitarian embrace; b) to be a demonstration of the Kingdom of God in human relationships, beliefs, and behavior; and c) to be the missionary arm of the Holy Trinity.[2]

Parenthetically, before we proceed further, it needs to be observed that the church is always incarnate in two different dimensions. One dimension is that of the church *gathered*, and it is this dimension that we will focus on in this Trail Guide. However, the other dimension is that the church is still the church when it is *scattered* into the warp and woof of daily life. It is that daily salt-and-light incarnation that makes it incumbent upon the church to be an equipping, nurturing, supportive community when it is gathered. The church is the Body of Christ no less on Thursday afternoon in the workplace or neighborhood than when it is gathered on the Lord's day, or whenever. We just need to be clear on that. If the church is truly a missional community, it must always be focused

---

1. See "Trail Guide #1."

2. I will insert, again, that what I am proposing for the underside church is also very germane to the rethinking of the whole traditional ecclesiology, and is therefore relevant to anyone thinking about the integrity and authenticity of the church as a vital component in the *missio dei*.

on being the incarnation of the mission of God in the neighborhood and in the world in which we live.

All that said, any community must have some form, however casual or intentional—so also our underside church. The wine always needs a wineskin! We usually tend to think in terms of *organization*—like time and place of meetings, plus inner-structure and responsibilities formally stated.[3] I want to shift the focus, rather, to *covenanted relationships* that are dynamically and encouragingly inter-animating, so much so that time and place are spontaneous (even casual, though intentional), missional, and as frequent as they are mutually feasible. (Is that a confusing statement, or what?) But that's the kind of flexible, versatile, and mobile form that I am advocating for these embedded refounding communities.[4]

These communities also need to have a very intentional *flavor*, or *character*, which will enable them to be the fragrance of the knowledge of Christ[5] in their ecclesiastical places of exile—or neighborhoods—even while their mission is "redemptively subversive."

In my own reading of the New Testament documents, I have extrapolated what I have discerned as, at least, eight essential characteristics, which give to the church its incarnational authenticity.[6] These are, admittedly, somewhat at odds with the classic definitions of the church found in most Christendom traditions. So be it. These signs are not listed in any priority since they are all inter-dependent and inter-animating as they become lived-out by the people of God. Here's the list:

---

3. The Christendom church is usually defined in terms of ecclesiastical authority, clergy, and sanctified buildings. We want to deliberatively set that whole concept aside. Such a Christendom ecclesiology is, to my way of thinking, a subversion of New Testament teaching (even though I, and we, live with inescapably within this millennium-and-a-half tradition).

4. Gerhard Lohfink, in his *Jesus And Community*, distinguishes between a *community* and a *society* in this regard—communities being more intimate and relational, and societies being more organizational and formal.

5. 2 Cor 2:15.

6. To be sure this is very much my personal discernment, and there may well be more things that are essential, but these are obvious to me and so I commend them to my readers.

1. The doxological character: glory of Father, Son, and Holy Spirit.
2. The empowering and dynamic presence of the Holy Spirit.
3. The passionate christological focus: "Worthy is the Lamb that was slain."
4. The Word of Christ dwelling richly within the New Creation community (and forming its life and behavior).
5. The primary work of the community: prayer (as communion with the God who calls and sends).
6. "One another" love: the relational character incarnating the love of God with each other according to the Great Commandment of Christ.
7. The radical and subversive thinking and behavior of God's Kingdom people: transformational praxis.
8. The mission of God: "As the Father has sent me, even so do I send you."

With these before us, let me pursue some brief guides to the a) *participation*, b) *form*, and c) *character* of the underside church in its mission of refounding the larger—and often forgetful—church institutions in which they are embedded.

PARTICIPATION

Before we go any further in these guides, we absolutely must look at the basic units of any community. Like, if one stops and ponders the whole concept of *the church*, it sooner or later becomes unavoidable to have to grapple with the subjects of the *who* and the *how* of participation in that same New Creation community. One must begin with the individuals who make up the community. Not only who makes up the community, but, also, what is their intent? What is their understanding of what they are getting into? How are they included or recognized? How are they formed and transformed into New Creation (or Kingdom of God) people? What is needed for them to be, self-consciously, *disciples* of Jesus Christ?

The Great Commission in the book of Matthew only says that Jesus instructed his followers to make disciples. He goes on to instruct them that these disciples are to be baptized and taught to observe all that Jesus has commanded them. Sounds good, but that leaves a whole lot unsaid.

Who are the models of all of these things: Kingdom understanding and Kingdom praxis? How does one learn to function relationally as New Creation (or Kingdom) folk? Christendom church institutions tend to be content with "church membership," but they also tend to be a bit light on anything that approaches the requirements (demands?) of discipleship. But, if our calling is as radically counter-cultural and missionally focused as we discussed (in the last Trail Guide on cosmology) . . . then even an initial consideration of identifying with such a counter-cultural community should be approached with some sobriety.

In the classic Rule of St. Benedict, which spells out some basic guides for that Roman Catholic Benedictine order, I find interesting wisdom. According to this Rule, one who is curious about monastic life approaches a chapter of the Order of St. Benedict as an "inquirer." For a time, he is immersed in the life and discipline and self-understanding that defines the mission of the order. If, after a time of such inquiry, one determines that he wishes to become a part of the order, he may be received into the chapter as a "novice," and begin a course of instruction and discipline necessary to make a life commitment. When the master of the novices is persuaded that a particular individual understands the discipline and has learned the rules, liturgies, rites, and relationships of the order—and will be a faithful and fruitful participant—only then may he be recommended for inclusion. Such inclusion, remember, is into a lifetime of commitment to the purpose, devotion, and mission of the order, and by virtue of his inclusion he then places himself under the oversight of the chapter and the abbot.

I am willing to propose that the underside church can learn from such deliberateness. While being very open in terms of those persons who are searching—and really do need to see the gospel in flesh and blood community—the community does need, at the same time, to be intentional and quite self-conscious in its focus on that *disciple-making* by which we are together formed into the image of Christ.

To that end I am willing to employ the eight characteristics above as applicable to individuals as well as to the community. Learning to authentically incarnate such New Testament priorities is a good, rule-of-the-thumb guide for the individuals who will make up the community that also incarnates these characteristics. In the next Trail Guide, we will take a look at God's provision for equipping such a community. For now, let me just insist that, while there is no inflexible formula for the sequence of baptism and disciple-making and teaching such as Jesus commands in Matthew 28, they are all part of the critical and formative process of inclusion into God's eschatological and transformational community of the New Creation.

FORM

The *form* of our underside church will be defined by the sixth characteristic of authenticity in the above list of eight. It is the one that highlights *one another love*. The very form, which makes such one-another relationships within the New Creation community possible, requires some set of intentional and covenanted relationships between the participants. One cannot engage in the redemptive intimacy of such mutual caring in a larger and more impersonal context. To *love one another as Christ has loved us* cannot be approached superficially or with any interpersonal detachment. It requires that we know the *names*, *faces*, and *stories* of those very real persons with whom we are engaged. It will require some networks of responsibility and accountability for each other. The New Testament teachings about our one-another ministries of caring are inescapable. This is what makes that one-another love characteristic the key to the form our underside community.

The form of such a community may be, in reality, somewhat porous and flexible, so that folk are free to be a part for a season, to "sniff it out," and, then, with the blessing of the community, to move on to other covenanted relationships. Or such a community, as it grows, may of necessity spawn other communities in order to maintain the integrity of the ministry and mission. One thing we must recognize, however, about our quest to refound the church from the underside, is that such a journey probably should never be engaged in alone—indeed, it cannot be. Jesus' *ecclesia* (church) is a calling into a New Creation *community*.

Referring back to the earlier illustration of my friend Jennifer (at the beginning of this study), and her intention to spend those several months on the Appalachian Trail . . . it involved others, sometimes intentional, sometimes accidental, on the same journey. It was not good or sensible or safe to be alone for too long in the wilderness of those hundreds of miles. So it is with us, as those who are called to be the community of the children of light, on our missional journey of faithfulness, in the midst of the dominion of darkness.

From the creation accounts in the book of Genesis, we see that God knew the need for the human community: "It is not good for man that he should be alone."[7] And even though this was spoken, at that point, about the creation of the male-female, husband-wife community, still the principle recurs throughout the Scriptures, and is a reflection of the trinitarian community. That trinitarian community is one of inter-animating and interpenetrating mutual relationships of love. The New Creation community, then, is to have the flavor of mutuality in accountability and responsibility and understanding and purpose. At the heart of such are not so much organizations but relationships defined of mutual purpose, encouragement, love and trust.

This form, of necessity, requires that it be quite small. Remember that one of Jesus' initial statements about the community, which he was in process of creating, was, "Where two or three are gathered in my name . . . ."[8] So, as we are looking at the form of the underside community within the larger church institution, underscore the principle that community and organization are not synonymous. There is a significant difference between a *society* and a *community*. A community is a composite of persons in relationships of redemptive love, mutuality, and caring.[9]

Our thesis in this whole study is that the purpose of the church, among other things, is to demonstrate God's new creation, or re-creation, of the human community into its true and original intent. As such it is to be a communal demonstration of *true community*, i.e., Kingdom community, which is visible to those outside. "By this shall all people know that you are my disciples, if you have love for one another."[10] Jesus taught this to his disciples in the context of his assertion that they were to love one another even as he had loved them.

Such love in relationships has an essential component of intimacy that cannot be achieved in a larger, impersonal society, or a church institution, even though such institutions may affirm the necessity of such love. As I said above, *community* requires that we know each other's names and faces and stories. Up front, it requires that we spend some significant time together in a setting that fosters such. It also requires

---

7. Gen 2:18.
8. Matt 18:20.
9. See Lohfink, *Jesus And Community*.
10. John 13:35.

that we accept a mutual and sensitive responsibility for each other and accountability to each other. Such New Creation community demonstrates the divine nature in its relational life together.

This being so, our underside community exists, within the larger and more impersonal church institution, both as a leavening influence and as a demonstration of New Creation community that is both visible and redemptive. I say this because, however well-intentioned the larger church institutions may be, it is all to easy for one to get lost in them, to be unintentionally a "non-person," or to be unaccountable to any other, or to be devoid of responsibility for any other of the brothers and sisters—or for the mission of God. Such community certainly cannot be another program for the church. Such communal authenticity cannot be taught in a class on "small groups," though the way may be pointed or appetites whetted for such.

In the church's mission in the world, this may explain the current data that indicates that the fastest growing edge of the church in the world today is caused by the proliferation of *house churches*. House churches require a minimum of organization, but are dependent upon the dynamic faith of the participants, and the authenticity of the relationships within. They are contagious because they are not seen as ecclesiastical institutions, but rather as homes, where there is hospitality and where folk meet with a common and contagious love for each other and a faith in Jesus as the Word of God made flesh and blood. This is all to say that the *new wine* of the gospel does, indeed, necessitate a wineskin—there does need to be some identifiable form for such New Creation communities as we are talking about. At the same time, our underside church form needs to be flexible, versatile, mobile, and viable to accomplish its purpose.

It was Paul who identified the church as the dwelling place of God by the Spirit.[11] In another place, he catalogs some of the fruits of the Spirit which demonstrate the divine nature dwelling within the lives of God's people . . . and, please note, those "fruits" are all relational. The fruits of the Holy Spirit indicate the redemptive character of our relationships with each other as real—and sometimes difficult and obstreperous—brothers and sisters within this New Creation community.[12] I say they are relational and I think that is true, but it may depend on our translations how this comes through. Take note: the fruits are *love, joyfulness,*

---

11. Eph 2:22.
12. Gal 5:22–23.

peaceableness, patience, kindness, goodness, faithfulness, gentleness, and self-control[13]—all relational, all expressed in the context of a one-another community. They reflect the divine nature expressing itself in the lives of God's sons and daughters.

CHARACTER OF THE UNDERSIDE CHURCH COMMUNITY

The *character* of the underside community will be the incarnation of those other seven characteristics of authenticity listed above. So let me walk you through them, and describe them briefly, even if incompletely. Each of them is essential and needs to have flesh and blood demonstration through our underside community if we are to be agents of refounding the larger church institutions into viable missional churches. When the gospel is obscured by the forgetfulness, mindlessness, and institutional idolatry—not to mention cultural insensitivity—that form so many congregations, what is required of our subversive underside community is the gentle, but urgent, inner witness that will remind them of their God given purpose, their teleology, as communities of the Kingdom of God.

The Doxological Character:
Glory of Father, Son, and Holy Spirit.

In an earlier work of mine,[14] I have already extrapolated seven characteristics of authenticity (of the eight listed above), but I failed to include this *doxological* characteristic that I am determined to put first here. In that earlier work, I failed to note that it is essential for the people of God that their lives together always be doxological—that they always be self-consciously given to the glory of the Triune God in their one-another lives as community, as well as in their daily lives in the very real world. Sound simple? Yes, but it is so easily displaced by preoccupation with ecclesiastical "stuff." The New Testament documents, as well as the great hymns of the church, are profoundly formed by such a doxological focus. But the Enlightenment, not to mention our current "consumer culture" churches, made the Christian faith so much more subjective—so much more focused on "my salvation" and my experiences of faith—that the

---

13. Ibid.
14. *Enchanted Community*.

focus subtly shifted, from the glory of the God of salvation, to us as the recipients of that salvation.

One of the great strengths of the classic liturgies of the church is that they still remembered that worship began with a focus on God, on adoration (not on *me* and *us*!). We see this in the *Te Deum laudamus* in such liturgies. So I have added this essential doxological characteristic of the authentic New Creation community and have placed it at the beginning of the list—just as a reminder to myself, if for nobody else.

The Empowering and Dynamic Presence of the Holy Spirit

Any thoughtful person will quickly discern, as he or she reads the New Testament documents, that one does not even begin to understand the mission of God, or the church of Jesus Christ apart from the dynamic presence of the Holy Spirit—one doesn't even *begin* to understand it apart from the Spirit of the Father and the Son who is to inhabit the church. Jesus made it quite plain to his disciples that what he was calling them to be, and to do, was humanly impossible. "Apart from me you can do nothing."[15] "Nevertheless I tell you the truth: it is for your advantage that I go away, for if I do not go away, the Helper will not come to you."[16] . . . He ordered them not to depart from Jerusalem, but to "wait for the promise of the Father . . . but you will be baptized with the Holy Spirit not many days from now . . . but you will receive power when the Holy Spirit has come upon you."[17]

It became the more obvious when the ascended Lord told one of the brothers, named Ananias, to go to the house of Judas in Damascus and to baptize Saul of Tarsus. He was then to promise Saul that he would regain his eyesight and "be filled with the Holy Spirit." This became the more revealing, later, when Saul, by then Paul, gave his own testimony of his commission from the Lord at that time, which was, "I am sending you to open their eyes, so that they may turn from darkness to light and *from the power of Satan to God*" (italics mine).[18] The missionary mandate, under which Paul and the church exist to this day, is absolutely ridiculous when conceived as a merely human enterprise.

---

15. John 15:5.
16. John 16:7.
17. Acts 1:4, 8.
18. Acts 26:1–18.

One can recruit church members without the power of the Spirit, but one certainly cannot open the eyes of the spiritually blind without that power. One would not even dare engage the powers of darkness apart from that Spirit presence. The book of Acts and the New Testament letters testify to this utter dependence upon the Holy Spirit . . . and how, when the Spirit was quenched, the work came to a halt.

Therefore, I am bold enough to say that a requisite characteristic of the authentic New Creation community is this selfsame conscious dependence upon the dynamic presence of the Holy Spirit. It is as such that the church is the "dwelling place of God by the Holy Spirit," as Paul describes the church in Ephesians.[19] Which means that our underside communities, again, must be the demonstration of such Spirit-dependent and Spirit-empowered communities within their larger ecclesiastical institutions.

Is it any wonder that one of the primary prayers of the church, in its times of fruitfulness, has always been Come Holy Spirit! *Veni Creator Spiritus!*

The Passionate Christological Focus: "Worthy is the Lamb that was slain."

How quickly the church has always had its vision deflected to other things. Ever so subtly, the church's focus shifts to its inner life, or to arguments about this and that, to the affairs of their present context, or to their institutional success, and they have forgotten Jesus, whose obedience to the Father—whose life, death, and resurrection—effected this great salvation. Paul reminded his young friend Timothy, with classic brevity, "Remember Jesus Christ . . ."[20] The early church at Laodacea had evidently become so wonderfully successful and preoccupied with their inner life that they left Jesus outside the door. In the letter to that church, Revelation 3, we find Jesus outside, knocking at the gate and seeking to be invited in again, so that he might have fellowship with his own people.

So much of the Christendom church becomes so idolatrous about its sanctuaries, so focused on its clergy, so consumed with doctrinal debates, so captivated by its ecclesiastical accoutrements, and so indifferent to its mission . . . that it becomes forgetful of Jesus. I, personally, encoun-

19. Eph 2:22.
20. 2 Tim 2:8.

tered this phenomenon early in my brief career engaging with major theological schools in this country. I noticed that, for all of the intellect and gifts of so many, there was far too often, in their chapel services, almost no mention of Jesus! Pride of theology, skill in liturgics, commendable homiletical exercises—but no consuming passion for Jesus.

Our underside church must always be a witness to the reality of the primary place, in its life together, of the Lamb of God. It must never become too preoccupied with other things to sing the song of heaven: "Worthy is the Lamb who was slain, to receive power and wealth and wisdom and might and honor and glory and blessing."[21] Not only must this adoration be at the heart of our communal times together, but also it becomes a significant part of our role in refounding the larger church institution, namely that of encouraging that institution out of its forgetfulness and its often displacing of Jesus with a multitude of activities.

And, by the way, the glorifying of the Son is also an evidence of the Holy Spirit among us: "He will glorify me . . ."[22]

The Word of Christ Dwelling Richly Within, and Forming the Community

A very basic question is this: What dynamic critical factor gives the New Creation community its form and character? What transformational power gives to it its authenticity as the Body of Christ, or the dwelling place of God by the Spirit? What is the content and common understanding that creates the mind of Christ within a community? Is there some divine lodestar that keeps God's people from wandering off into some subversion that is inimical to the great eschatological design of God?

Absolutely. Let me respond to these questions with an observation or two. It is always a bit disturbing to me, that for all of the Christendom church institution's ecclesiastical life, how easily it forgets a basic commandment of Jesus. Even missional-minded communities, who often speak of the Great Commission, seem to forget a significant part of that commission. Remember that Jesus' commission had several components: 1) All authority is given to me; 2) Go *make disciples* of all peoples; 3) Baptize them in the name of the Father and of the Son and of the Holy Spirit. It is what follows, the fourth component, that is the focus of my first observation: *Teach them to observe all that I have*

---

21. Rev 5:12.
22. John 16:14.

commanded you. Consider the content and implications of that part of the commandment.

This is followed by the assurance that, in this humanly impossible mission, to which Jesus is calling his church, Jesus, himself, will be with his people even unto the end of the age. My second observation may be a bit more subtle, and yet it is so obvious if we can get rid of our traditional filters. Remember that Jesus spent a couple of years with this fairly small group of disciples in all kinds of situations and challenges, but he was teaching them, all the time, about who he was and what he came to do in the great search-and-rescue-mission of God. He modeled before them what he was teaching. So much was this so, that when he came to this point, at the end of his earthly ministry, he could, in essence, say, "Okay, guys, what I have been doing with you, teaching you, showing you—now it's your turn. Go out to all the people groups of the world and do the same thing." That's called *disciple making.* That's intentional engagement that transforms individuals and communities with New Creation thinking and behavior.

It follows, then, that out of this Great Commission these two pieces are intimately connected. If I can state these two pieces in the form of questions: First, what does it mean to *make disciples*? And, second, what is the content of *teaching them to observe all that I have commanded you*? Somehow, at the most basic interpretation of this, making disciples means orienting those who believe in Jesus and his New Creation into the counter-cultural life and thinking and behavior patterns—not to mention the demonstration of divine power in engaging the darkness—of that new relationship and reality.

Jesus was literally reproducing himself in the lives of his followers. That meant spending time with these folk and modeling, teaching, coaching, mentoring, equipping, and encouraging them, until Christ be formed in them. That was done, not in some spiritual (ecclesiastical?) isolation, but in the realities of their contemporary culture. Paul will later say to the Philippian believers: "What you have learned and received and heard and seen in me—practice these things, and the God of peace will be with you."[23] That gives us the strong flavor of disciple making.

But then Jesus gave us a most critical dimension of this formation of disciple making. He instructed the eleven disciples to be teaching these baptized persons to observe, or practice, all that he had commanded

---

23. Phil 4:9.

them. What's that all about? At the very least, from within Matthew's gospel document, a commentator like Frederick Dale Bruner has discerned six sermons that cover the whole of Jesus' messianic teaching of the life and behavior of the Kingdom. They deal significantly with the meaning of discipleship, missions and evangelism, parables on the Word of God, congregational ethics, and the last things and last judgment.[24] Needless to say, appropriating and observing these teachings would go a long way to forming any communal understanding—yet I seldom hear that part of the Great Commission encouraged. There is too often some kind of endemic vacuousness and mindlessness in all too many who profess church membership.

Next, let me point you to the passage in Colossians in which Paul writes to this community of believers, "Let the word of Christ dwell among you richly, *teaching and admonishing one another* in all wisdom, singing psalms and hymns and spiritual songs, with thankfulness in your hearts to God" (italics mine).[25] What is indicated in this passage is that, in their small fellowship (note the one-another dimension of this), there is to be such a common passion for the word of Christ that the participants can actually be formative factors in each other's lives. But such a mutual ministry requires that there be that common knowledge of the word of Christ, somehow existing dynamically and transformationally, in their lives together.[26]

Such an apostolic exhortation can never be realized significantly in a large, somewhat impersonal church institution with a twenty-five minute sermon-monologue out of a pulpit—though even that would be most encouraging if the pulpit were actually contagious with a passion for scripture!

The reference in Colossians 3:16–17 needs to be inscribed deeply in the heart of the underside church, so much so that it becomes contagious into the larger amnesiac church institution. The Spirit works powerfully through the Word of Christ to form and transform and equip the people

---

24. Frederick Dale Bruner's two volumes on Matthew are *The Christbook*, and *The Church Book*. My versions of this are now out of print, but it may now be reprinted in a single volume.

25. Col 3:16.

26. In the next Trail Guide, we will talk about the missional gifts of the Spirit that are given to equip God's people for their daily mission. Among them is the gift of the *teaching shepherd*, which I personally believe are those persons who are especially equipped to be teachers and expositors of the biblical documents.

of God, and must never be thought of as any kind of peripheral elective for some few curious folk. In an earlier Trail Guide, I quoted from Gerald Arbuckle about how the church, or missional order, reverts to chaos whenever it dilutes, displaces, or forgets its founding myth, i.e., that commonly held body of truth that brought it into being in the first place.

In the twenty-first century, we have polls that indicate that even within formidable church traditions there is widespread biblical and theological ignorance. The Scriptures are our story, and, as Walter Brueggemann has so effectively put it, "This story has come from somewhere and is going somewhere, and we can truly know where we are going only if we know where we have come from. In order to have vision we must have memory."[27] Note, however, that this is every believer's responsibility: to be a factor in the mutual ministry of Biblical formation, by which we become the Spirit's agents in keeping the mission of God focused in our lives together, as we seek to be also a leavening factor in the larger, and often forgetful, church institutions in which we are embedded.

The Primary Work of the Community: Prayer

Even as the New Creation community is to be formed by the Word of Christ, so its God-given mission is totally impossible unless empowered by the Spirit of God. The priority of prayer in the life and ministry of Jesus is quite obviously continued in the life and ministry of the post-pentecostal community. This primary work is most germane to what I am proposing here as the refounding ministry of the underside community. Ours is a totally different context than that of the first generation church found in the book of Acts—but the dynamics of creating communities of the Kingdom of God (New Creation) within the dominion of darkness are no less impossible unless empowered by the Spirit of God.

This brings us to an essential component in this process of forming such communities. It is probably most succinctly stated in Paul's word to the church in Ephesus: " . . . praying at all times in the Spirit, with all prayer and supplication."[28]

Consider that the God who comes to us in Jesus, who demonstrates New Creation (Kingdom) life before us in Jesus the word made flesh . . . the God who teaches us how to pray in Jesus, and who makes extravagant

---

27. Walsh and Keesmaat, *Colossians Remixed*, 134.
28. Eph 6:18.

promises to us about the efficacy of prayer . . . who also indicates that it is not only, nor primarily, a solitary discipline[29] . . . is quite obviously the God who not only knows we need to be in communication with him, but *wants* to be in communication with us . . . who as our father wants to equip and empower us for the humanly impossible mission for which he call us, and to which he sends us.

On our part, we absolutely need to know, at the very least, 1) the mind of God, 2) the will of God, and 3) the power of God, in all of the earthly, and human, and social-cultural realities and vicissitudes that we meet, expectedly and unexpectedly, each day. Or consider the sobering potential of God's calling a bunch of flawed and imperfect persons such as we, with all of the remnants of autonomy still clinging to us . . . "out of the dominions of darkness and into the Kingdom of his dear Son."[30] It should drive us to prayer.

What one finds, then, as we observe the church in the New Testament documents—this New Creation community and mission, being birthed and launched into a hostile and rebellious world—is a community not only being formed radically new by the Word of Christ (above) . . . but also, of necessity, engaging in a continual communion with their risen Lord through prayer, this One who has promised to be with them in this mission, even unto the end of the age.

The New Testament documents do not ever speak of worship services, or of any institutional establishment, or of most of the things that we in the twenty-first century identify as the "necessary" components of the church. Rather, we find the believers in Christ gathering in the presence of the God who has called them into this newness, praying their way through decisions, dangers, persecutions, internal conflicts, and challenges. We find them praying and fasting (and as a result, sending their leaders off on a missionary journey!). And, interestingly, we find the church spontaneously and dramatically growing into neighboring regions—like leaven!

In short, the primary *work* of the New Creation community—and, hence, of our underside community—is missionary obedience birthed in prayer. Out of their life of prayer together, they discerned the mission and were empowered for it. It was in their prayers that they were formed to be Christ's faithful witnesses, beginning right where they were. It was

29. Cf. Matt 18:19–20, John 14:13–14, etc.
30. See Col 1:13.

in prayer that the Spirit opened their eyes to see those next door . . . and those to the uttermost parts of the earth. How and where did these prayers take place? However or wherever is hardly our concern. They prayed when they were together! Again, the form of the church is quite versatile, and is mostly a one-another configuration.

Once again, we are attempting to extrapolate from the biblical documents something of the flesh-and-blood flavor of their communal prayers. So much of our Christendom church concept is somewhat skewed by our own experience of a group of individual Xs (church members) sitting in a circle and praying for some mutually agreed upon Ys (causes outside) in some fairly safe, traditional setting, for maybe thirty minutes, or perhaps longer. But consider that the first generation church, about which we read in the New Testament, was in a totally new and untested and unknown setting that was frequently illegal. They would have been praying for what?

Because they usually operated in some house-to-house form, and because they were *all* engaged in the mission (ministry), they would of necessity have been praying for each other, for the discernment of each other's gifts and ministries, since each was understood to have such an active role in this household of faith.[31] Before God's throne of grace, they would have been praying for each other's responsibilities and accountabilities in and for this mission. They would have been praying for the practical realities of their inner lives.

They would also be praying for their contact and communication with those persons with whom they were engaged outside the household of faith. They would have been resisting passivity in their New Creation lives, and calling for the power of God to energize them to be the demonstration of that New Creation before the watching world. And their sensitive love for each other would call forth prayers for the practical realities that were the individual and familial lives of each.

Evangelism, church planting, mission, transformed lives, healings, engagement with real principalities and powers . . . are all impossible without prayer. Closer to home there were the impoverished, the sick and infirm, the demon possessed, and all those expressions of the brokenness of the dominion of darkness. Factor in that they had only their meager resources humanly—but they had access to the power and the resources of their divine father as they were about his work of preaching

---

31. See the next Trail Guide on the equipping gifts and the household gifts.

the gospel, healing the sick, feeding the hungry, cleansing the lepers, and casting out demons . . . through them.[32]

The church invented itself in prayer as it went along.

For us, so much of the amnesiac church, in which we underside folk operate, doesn't anticipate divine intervention, serious engagement with neighbors in darkness (souls in bondage), major gospel-out-of-control breakouts into whole new and humanly unreachable ethnic and generational cultures. So why should we bother to pray?

It is worth noticing that, in Paul's word about the necessity of the "whole armor of God" if we are to stand or survive in the evil day, he concludes with the often neglected necessity of praying at all times in the Spirit.[33] One hymn writer has called this "the trustiest weapon of all."[34] There is a sense in which our calling is so totally impossible, that we are always *praying against the impossible* in our pilgrimage.

If we factor in such passages as Hebrews 2:2–4 (" . . . the message declared by angels . . . declared first by the Lord . . . and attested to us by those who heard him, while *God also bore witness by signs and wonders and various miracles and gifts of the Holy Spirit . . .*" [italics mine]), then, again, we are definitely not looking at some merely human effort. We are praying with expectation of divine response in ways beyond our asking or imagining.

All of this speaks to our journey into refounding the church from the underside. As it was with the first generation church, so it is with us. Prayer becomes our primary work. Prayer is the language of communication with Father, Son, and Holy Spirit, within the embrace of the Trinitarian community. In prayer, we become intimate with the Trinitarian community in our calling to be the Trinity's missionary arm. In prayer, we see our lives and mission through God's eyes.

The realities of our amnesiac church institutions is that these particular ecclesiastical mission fields are likewise often inhabited by those in deep bondage to the darkness, albeit a spiritual darkness . . . and they are unaware of it. They are captive to ecclesiastical principalities

---

32. I would not be surprised if the reason that, by far, most of the prayer concerns voiced in our Christendom churches have to do with illness and catastrophic happenings . . . is because these are the areas where we meet our human helplessness. Whereas almost everything else we do in such churches is the product of our human efforts: recruiting members, running the institution, raising the budget, etc. Just a thought!

33. Eph 6:10–18.

34. Montgomery, "Behold! The Christian Warrior Stands."

and powers, to religious darkness, to "another gospel" of institutional pride and success. This is what necessitates "the trustiest weapon of all"—prayer. Blind eyes *inside* the church must be opened, and this only happens through prayer.

With the church in the book of Acts, their journey was into a hostile world. With us, our journey is within the mission field of amnesiac church institutions. Like that early church, so we also know that blind eyes, deaf ears, unresponsive hearts, gospel indifference, satisfaction with institutional reputation and success, and obliviousness, somewhat, to the mission of God to seek and to save the lost . . . and more . . . is only responsive to persistent prayer: *Come Holy Spirit!*

The Radical and Subversive Thinking and Behavior of God's Kingdom People: Transformational Praxis.

I have chosen the terminology for this particular characteristic quite intentionally. It actually comes from the not-at-all subtle teaching of the Sermon on the Mount, which sermon is of the essence of the lifestyle and ethic of the people of the Kingdom of God. The Sermon on the Mount is an amazing document. It is also anything but tame and safe and "spiritual." It is, rather, an *in-your-face* counter-cultural challenge to the values and culture of the Roman Empire, to a forgetful Jewish establishment, and to the pagan Greek culture in which the church was called.

The Beatitudes are anything but a sweet set of spiritual inanities. The culture in which those first followers of Jesus lived was probably not too unlike so much of our own, what with economic injustice and helpless poverty, ever-present suffering, loss, and hopelessness; the pride and arrogance and maybe self-righteousness of the leaders, along with greed and mammon worship. Add to those an indifference to justice and ethics, frequent cruelty and merciless dealings, dubious motives, double-mindedness, lack of authenticity and transparency, strife, conflict, warfare, violence persecution of all who would interfere or not compromise with this dominant culture, not to mention character assassination.

Read into that context, the Beatitudes are the exact opposite, and they indicate that persecution may well await those who seek to live out those Kingdom characteristics. Remember, too, that these Beatitudes are nothing less than the divine nature indwelling God's New Creation people and demonstrating God's own nature in human affairs. That much for starts.

If the Christian community is to be formed by the Word of Christ, then, so also is the behavior and thinking of God's Kingdom people. It is with this in mind, then, that Jesus concludes just these initial principles, of this larger teaching, with the critical necessity of living them out in visible flesh and blood lives. He tells his disciples that this is what makes them salt and light in the human community. He warns that if they don't demonstrate this kind of Kingdom behavior and thinking, then they are essentially worthless. It is by their being the children of light in the midst of cultural and social darkness that the world actually sees what God is doing in the world.

But the word that follows here is so very essential to our thesis in our refounding mission. It is not religious *talk* that is effective. Paul would later say that our gospel does not come just in words, but in power. Here Jesus tells us that it is what the watching world *sees* in us that makes known the glory of God: "In the same way, let your light shine before others, so that they may see your good works and give glory to your Father who is in heaven."[35] I will not belabor this characteristic of authenticity that must adorn our underside community in its mission. It must be the sweet aroma of Christ in the midst of what can often be discouraging, sterile church institutions. It must demonstrate thoughtful, wise, gracious, humble, loving . . . but intentional New Creation intelligence and behavior—and such intelligence and behavior, count on it, is *radical* and *subversive.*

Our own particular refounding journey is taken in a society dominated by a consumer culture, and an entertainment culture. More than we like to admit, too many of our church institutions become captive to that culture, and so *commodify* their message and their institutions, to conform to such a dominant consumer and entertainment culture. Even as the Roman Empire dared anyone to challenge or embarrass the empire, so this culture surely seeks to intimidate any who stand in missionary confrontation with its superficiality and darkness.

All you have to do is to keep allowing the Word of Christ to dwell richly in your midst and you will find yourself living out responses and lifestyles that challenge the dominant culture, both ecclesiastical and secular. Living in this already-but-not-yet Kingdom of God will bring us frequently into some ambiguity about many things, but not about God's design to demonstrate his New Creation through us. People will take our

35. Matt 5:16.

words seriously when they see lives that somehow reflect something that whets their appetites to know more.

Such Kingdom thinking and behavior may begin with our taking our neighbors seriously as real and precious human persons, and not dehumanizing them, or ignoring them, as is so much the pattern in all too much of the society in which we live.

The Mission of God: "As the Father has sent me, even so do I send you."

One of the tragedies of the Constantinian subversion of the church—and its ultimate formation as Christendom—was that the church became a *location* and an *institution* rather than being a mobile and versatile missional movement. To put it another way, the church became "landed," or "at home," in a place of security. Part of that, also, as we have said earlier, is that we created institutions that were hierarchical and clergy-focused, so that the vast majority of the baptized folk did not see themselves as essential to the mission of God. Somehow, in this subtle drift from missional community to institution, the New Creation community also forgot its teleology, and therefore ceased to equip *all* of God's people to be fruitful in the mission to which Jesus has called his church.

The empire co-opted the church, and few noticed. Thinking and behavior were no longer, necessarily, formed by the Word of Christ. The teaching shepherds of Ephesians 4:11 were redefined as priests, and became the *sacralized* persons responsible for maintaining the institution for those inside, and thereby becoming all too oblivious to those outside. Perhaps the greatest tragedy of this, in terms of the mission of God, was that the church became *clergified*, and thereby rendered the laity to a passive role as merely participants and supporters of the clergy. The church ceased to equip all of God's people for their participation in the mission. It forgot that the gifts of the Spirit were given to all of Christ's followers.

This was an enormous subversion. And that becomes the subject of our next Trail Guide. At this point in our journey, any thoughtful or pragmatic person is going to ask, How does this happen? Who equips for such *radically other*, or counter-cultural, salt-and-light living? Where does one find the models, or receive the Word of Christ, or participate in a transformational context that makes all of this real? We will pursue these questions in the next Trail Guide.

But . . . for now, I need to underscore that these eight characteristics *together* give the New Creation community its authenticity, and when any one of them is missing, or diminished, the design of God for his church is diminished.

SPECIFICS FOR THE TRAIL

As a basic guideline for some sort of a covenanted relationship for any underside cohort, one might consider simply using these eight characteristics as the basis for the relationship between those participating. This would give something of a simple goal for their lives together, no matter how casual and non-scheduled it might be. This would be like any ad hoc group traversing a trail, who agreed that such-and-such was to be our destination, without knowing, exactly, all that might be involved in the process.

Trail Guide # 5

The Spirit's Formation and Furnishing of the Missional Community[1]

At this point in our journey, we come to one of the more complex, controversial, and thrilling components in our understanding of the design of God for his New Creation community, which will be critical for our understanding of our ministry of refounding. It has to do with how we are to understand the *inner dynamics*—maybe the *Spirit-dynamics*—of our life together in our missional journey. Please understand that a pervasive Christendom fog of misunderstanding makes this particular Trail Guide quite difficult to communicate. It is also here that we encounter, in all of its subverting, and scarcely noticed, and filtering effectiveness, the Christendom legacies of the institutionalization and clergification of the church.[2]

When the church, over those post-Constantinian generations, shifted its self-conscious focus from being a dynamic and mobile mission movement, into being settled and focused on sacralized buildings (sanctuaries), and a sacralized class of persons (called *priests* or *clergy*), and all of the liturgical rites that went along with that—something took place that has had an unfortunate, if not tragic, effect on the church's self-understanding and on the mission of God. A special place, and a special class of persons, redefined the church's mission and substituted

---

1. This Trail Guide will undoubtedly be the longest of all. If the truth were told, it was this concept that first provoked in my heart and mind this whole *underside church* journey. I find this one of the most overlooked and underestimated and critical pieces of the church's whole understanding of its nature and mission.

2. Missiologist Howard Snyder has written, semi-humorously, and communicated to me in personal conversation, that if you want to know how healthy your church is then "sell the building," to which I would add that we might either eliminate or radically redefine *clergy*!

for it a *Christendom ecclesiology*. It is this subversion and filter that complicates our desire to see our forgetful church institutions refounded.

Such a controversial concept, however, takes us back to our second characteristic of authenticity in the previous Trail Guide, namely the utter necessity and dynamic presence of the Holy Spirit in the formation of the New Creation community. It would seem that the biblical documents portray the church as the community through which God designs to recreate the human community into its original intent, and to embrace that human community (or church) once again within the trinitarian community. It is in that sense that Paul will speak of the Spirit as so empowering and inhabiting those who are his community that the church will be an expression of the glory of God, even as the Son is the agent of the glory of God.[3]

HOW DOES THIS HAPPEN?

The insistent question comes, then, as to exactly how this works itself out in the practical realities of our experience? How is such a community formed and equipped? Who does this? How does God literally recreate the human community so that every participant, every single rescued child of God, is an essential part of this selfsame demonstration of the thrilling news of the Kingdom of God? Where do we begin in our quest? What *filters* and *subversions* have deflected our focus onto some alien understanding of our calling, and of the church? How does the ecclesiastical legacy of Christendom become for us a major impediment—or severely limit our self-understanding, or subvert our God-given teleology? How does such an understanding become more than theory? Are there living examples of this being made real—or are we just talking to ourselves in some theoretical never-never-land?

In pursuit of our intended journey of refounding the church from the underside, I want to establish a vision of self-effacing, and somewhat hidden colonies, inhabiting existing Christendom church institutions, in all of their many traditions and forms. I would like to encourage these underside cohorts to change the way we "think church," and the way we "do church." I want to work on conceiving the church again in terms of *a missional movement in communal form*. I want to encourage such folk to see the church pragmatically, and as dynamically equipped by

---

3. Eph 3:21.

the Spirit for the task in each church's particular cultural-social context. Such an understanding will also require that churches be inventing and re-inventing themselves afresh, as they respond obediently to the Word and Spirit. Such leavening influence becomes one of the quiet roles of our underside communities.

After all, it is not that uncommon for venerable church institutions to have so *diluted*, or *displaced*, or *forgotten* altogether why the church exists in the first place, so that they are quite content with an ecclesiastical expression that has little to do with the Kingdom of God. In this Trail Guide, we will want to explore how it is, in the Scriptures, that we are pointed to the pragmatic and practical design. The ascended Lord Jesus gives to his church those gifts that actually and practically furnish and equip the New Creation community to faithfully carry out his mission—to demonstrate the inner dynamics of true community. Then, we purpose to attempt some helpful suggestions on how actual underside colonies might incarnate such a refounding influence in what so often appears to be a humanly impossible ecclesial scene.

We need to remind ourselves again of our premise. It is our understanding and conviction that the divine teleology for the church is that it is not only to be the community of God's New Creation, recreated to be the human community as God intended it to be . . . but that it is, by virtue of that, to be the visible demonstration of the very habitation of the divine nature—which divine nature is to be visible in the relationships and ministry that Christ's followers have with each other within that community. This necessitates, also, the presence of the power of God by the Spirit! It is not humanly achievable, please note.

This is not to diminish, in the least, that our underside church is to be the visible demonstration also, by the way in which it sees and expresses that divine nature and compassion for the whole of the larger human community, and the whole of God's creation. It is to be *salt and light* in its cultural context. The New Creation community is to create a veritable Kingdom culture, or counter-culture, replete with all of the wonder and mystery and beauty, and suffused with the divine nature and with all that such implies for this community . . . which after all, God intends to be the bride of Christ.

Then, add in the New Testament insight that the church is to be the "dwelling place of God by the Holy Spirit."[4] Such an awesome insight tells

---

4. Eph 2:22.

us that the church is inhabited by the Spirit of the Father and the Son, and is, therefore, within the embrace of the trinitarian community. The church is, by such an understanding, the *glory* of God—which is exactly what Paul has expressed in praying: "Now . . . to him be *glory in the church*, and in Christ Jesus throughout all generations . . ." (italics mine).[5]

Visible glory! Take a breath and digest that dynamic reality and its implications.

Jesus would hardly announce that he was irresistibly going to build his church . . . and then leave his hapless followers clueless to figure it out on their own, nor to wring their hands in ineptitude about what happens next. Nor did he give his commission[6] and leave us to figure how to make disciples of all the world's ethnic groups (or nations) on our own.

Remember, however, he did underscore several times that his merely human disciples were not going to be left on their own (orphans), with only their human resources to depend on. Jesus told them, very plainly, "Without me you can do nothing!" Jesus let them know that he had much more that was necessary to communicate to them, but that they simply couldn't handle it yet. Later, and when the Spirit would come, Jesus promised he would continue the enlightenment and empowerment.

He let them know that it was absolutely necessary for him to go away, so that the Holy Spirit should come, since they could never, never accomplish what he was calling them to do with their merely human resources—i.e., without such divine empowerment. All of which informs us that God, of necessity, provides the practical and empowering equipment necessary for the church to fulfill its eschatological design. That design was the creation of Christ's *church*, which was to be the missionary arm of the Trinity. It is to be the communal agent in the mission of God.

The church engages in that design by being the *visible* recreation of God's design, for the reconciled human community, and of redeemed relationships and inter-animating love. As such, it is to incarnationally declare the thrilling news of the Kingdom of God to the whole earth—to the watching world. Such must of necessity be fleshed out in the context of more limited and intimate communities, in which all of the participants are *interdependently* part of the Father's family, with names and faces and stories all known to each other, and sharing life with each other. It is designed to be a community of mutual responsibility and accountability.

5. Ibid., 3:20–21.
6. Matt 28.

∽ ∽ ∽

At the risk of (admitted) redundancy, let me stop here and make full disclosure to my readers, because this juncture presents challenges that some may not even want to engage—or may not be able to comprehend. I want to move beyond the horizons, or ecclesiastical definitions, within which we have been operating, and which have been formed over the past millennium and a half. This will not be easy or simple. The tentacles of the Christendom subversion run deep into our individual and corporate consciousness.

Specifically, I want to address the eclipse of the fascinating and awesome New Testament teachings concerning *the gifts and ministries of the Holy Spirit* within the New Creation community.

Such an eclipse—the eclipse of such a very prominent piece of New Testament instruction—seems unquestionably to have been related to the emergence of Christendom—at least, that is my conclusion. It was in that general Constantinian period that the emphasis of the church morphed from a *missional movement*, dependent upon the divine and dynamic empowerment and guidance of the Spirit, to an *ecclesial institution* that would be more humanly secure, permanent, and controllable . . . and not necessarily dependent upon the dynamic presence of the Spirit. When such a shift of self-understanding took place, over a period of generations, it became possible for the church to actually function, for all practical purposes, without the Spirit at all!

Somehow, in that general transition, the awesome provision of Spirit life and presence for the whole New Creation community, or church, made by the ascended Lord, became either displaced, or taken captive, or became the special preserve of the emerging priestly-clergy class. There were, of course, always those who were acknowledged leaders in the community, but a notion of *sacralized persons*, at least, became more pronounced during the general time frame of the third through the fifth centuries (more or less). I shall return to that later.

If the Holy Spirit is the one who creates the church, and who inhabits it, the question that follows is how, then, does the Holy Spirit equip and give form and order and dynamism and vitality to that community? The New Creation community, formed by the Holy Spirit, is only going to be authentic, and contagious, and inter-animating, and mutually ministering, and dynamic as it demonstrates the grace and love and wonder of the divine nature which inhabits it—and that habitation by the Spirit was to be expressing itself within and among *all* of its component folk.

My thesis here is that the church that is going to be the missionary arm of the Trinity is only going to be recognized, not by its institutional and organizational expressions of a Christendom sort, but rather by its demonstration of the divine nature that inhabits it and recreates it into God's eschatological design.[7] It is going to demonstrate, before the watching world, the very dynamics that are true within the trinitarian community. I offer here this quote from the theologian Colin Gunton on the relationships that exist within the trinitarian community as a pattern for us: ". . . the picture of divine love expressing itself even as those three Persons are *in* each other, *making room* for each other, *interpenetrating* and *interanimating* each other, *drawing life from* and *pouring life into* each other, and seeking the (consummate welfare and fulfillment) of each other . . . in eternity Father, Son, and Spirit share a dynamic and mutual reciprocity."[8]

I do not think it is at all unrealistic to understand that this same dynamic that exists within the trinitarian community is to be reflected in the daughters and sons of that same God as they dwell together in God's eschatological community of the New Creation. One has only to read such a thesis such as Paul's letter to the Ephesians to see this dynamic reflected on every page!

Saying that, however, does not mean that we can ignore the New Testament teachings that suggest to us how it is that God furnishes this church for both its *communal* and its *missional and practical* realities. And it is here that we arrive at the awesome working of the Spirit—the Spirit of the Father and the Son given to furnish the missional church. The Spirit is given to equip the church for its work of New Creation demonstration, and to animate that church with the very servant ministry that it is to demonstrate within this present context of darkness . . . as the salt of the earth and light of the world.

---

7. Remember that the church always inserts the caveat *provisionally* when it speaks of the church in the design of God. In this between-the-ages period, that recreation is always in process, hence *provisional*.

8. Quoted from my book *Enchanted Community* and its footnote to the magnificent work of Colin Gunton, *The One And The Three And The Many*.

∽ ∽ ∽

I need to explain to my readers that I have not found a great deal of assistance in much of the commentary on the New Testament, or the theological expressions of the church, except in some unique and non-traditional works (some Pentecostals, a few radical thinkers such as Jacques Ellul, some renegade Roman Catholics, and especially some theologians from the majority world of Latin America, Africa, and Asia!).[9] So what I am offering is not altogether original with me, but I do propose this thesis for my readers' consideration, quite aware of the resistance of all too much of the Christendom church, and too many of its teachers: The emergence of clergy seems to have muted what is the dynamic factor in communal life in the Spirit.

I want to propose that there appear to be at least—I see at least—three definable categories of Spirit-gifts (charismata) in the New Testament documents. They are what I will term *missional (or equipping) gifts*, *household gifts*, and *leadership gifts*.[10] Let me explain what I see.

If the church is to be the reconciled and recreated human community as God designs the human community to be . . . (including all the aromas of pure-hearted love, wonder, music, hope, redemptive relationships, mutually-edifying conversation, compassion, the doing of justice, the heralding of the Reign of God inaugurated by Jesus Christ, etc.) . . . if it is to be the dwelling place of God by the Spirit, if it is to be the missionary arm of the Holy Trinity, if it is to effectively demonstrate God in Christ to the watching world . . . then, one must inescapably ask *how* the Spirit effectively equips and furnishes and empowers this same dwelling place, by the Spirit, in flesh and blood reality? How in communal relationships? How in Kingdom living and thinking? How in leadership and examples of grace, humility, love, wisdom, formed in knowledge of the Word of Christ? How does one learn how to be, and how to live life within, such a New Creation community?

---

9. While writing this I had recommended to me by a fresh-thinking church planter the recent work by Viola and Barna, *Pagan Christianity*, which really rocked my ecclesiology!

10. The fruits of the Spirit, found in Galatians 5, are a different category, but also are the relational energizings of the Spirit within the community. More later.

Unless we come to grips with this dynamic furnishing of the community by the Holy Spirit, our Trail Guide will lead us off into a dead-end of more-of-the-same, Christendom-formed church, and not into the communal and missional dimensions of God's New Creation, God's Kingdom.

MISSIONAL, OR EQUIPPING, OR DISCIPLE-MAKING GIFTS (EPHESIANS 4:1–16)

My conviction is that the church, as God's reconciled and recreated New Creation human community, is never, never conceived of, nor intended to be, a static and passive ecclesiastical institution, such as we have made it to be in Christendom. Rather, as has come dramatically to light—especially under the influence of missiologist Lesslie Newbigin[11]—the church is to be self-consciously and dynamically a *missional community*. There are all kinds of telling implications to such a concept. To conceive the church, as such, returns the church to being a missional movement in communal form, rather than an institution with, maybe, a missionary program tacked on.[12]

Once the church is so conceived, then one's eyes are opened to the fact that the New Testament is primarily the guidebook for the nature and dynamics of God's mission in Christ, and through his church. That church is intended to be a versatile, flexible, mobile, and dynamic movement that takes on communal form as it goes, but never becomes passive about its mandate to make disciples of every ethnic group in the world, until "this gospel of the kingdom has been proclaimed in every nation . . ."[13] It is not surprising, then, that we find spelled out in the New Testament documents God's provisions for the furnishing of such a missional community by the Holy Spirit. After all, Jesus promised that when

---

11. Within the last half-century, no one has so challenged the thinking of the Christian church as the British missiologist Lesslie Newbigin. After nearly a half-century as a missionary and bishop in South India, Newbigin came home to the UK, only to find that it was much more difficult to express the Christian gospel in Christendom England than it was in primarily Hindu India. Out of his fertile heart and mind came books such as *Foolishness To The Greeks*, and *The Gospel In A Pluralistic Society* (along with many others). His challenge has called forth fresh missional thinking in both Protestant and Catholic circles. I need to celebrate his contribution here.

12. I think it was missiologist Howard Snyder who made this observation—somewhere I picked it up and have appreciated it.

13. Matt 24:14.

the Spirit should come, then all of the realistic dynamics of carrying out his calling, and his eschatological design, would be made known and provided for his followers.[14]

The absolute, and unequivocal, and critical necessity would be the dynamic Presence of the Holy Spirit. Every person who was called to follow Jesus became, by virtue of his or her baptism, empowered to become part of Christ's missional movement and a functioning member of this Spirit-inhabited community. This means that it is critical for our discussion here to realize that such a community is *not* a natural, or a *merely human*, community. It has an unmistakable divine and supernatural and enchanted essence to it—even though it is composed of human members fraught with all kinds of potential for reverting-to-type, and, in so doing, thereby operating on merely human principles.[15]

So, then . . . how would a person who had become a follower of Jesus through repentance and faith then be formed and fashioned, so that he or she could function authentically and fruitfully in such a Spirit-community? How would they be equipped to minister to one another in the Spirit, and in the context of the dominion of darkness, i.e., the *world*, which is also their place of habitation? How would they be equipped to be functioning members of such a missional community?

What (in the words of this text) would be necessary for them to be *". . . equipped for the work of ministry, for the building up of the Body of Christ, until they all attain to the unity of the faith and the knowledge of the son of God, to maturity, to the measure of the stature of the fullness of Christ, so that they be no longer children, tossed to and fro by waves, and carried about by every wind of teaching, by human cunning, by craftiness in deceitful schemes . . . but rather speaking the truth in love, they speak the truth in love, and grow up in every way into him who is the head, into Christ, from whom the whole body, joined together by every joint with which it is equipped, when each part is working properly, and the body grows and builds itself up in love . . ."*?[16]

---

14. John 16:4–15.

15. Let me repeat this just so that it doesn't get lost: The church's teachers and theologians have used the term "provisional" to indicate the incomplete and in-process nature of our individual and corporate lives as God's New Creation folk. So the church is *provisionally* the demonstration of God's New Creation community.

16. Eph 4:11–16.

How? Whose responsibility? I'm going to ask that you indulge me a hermeneutical, or interpretative, risk here. Better still, allow me to engage in a *missional and pneumatic hermeneutic*. I've done a reasonable bit of study and biblical exegesis on this Ephesians text, and I must admit that most of the commentaries are frustrating, simply because they avoid, or deal unconvincingly, with the whole import of the *charisms*, or gifts, of the Spirit to the church. They seem to have put a "Christendom spin" or interpretation on the text. It seems that the Christendom expression of the church has created a whole ecclesiology that easily displaces these gifts with its own concepts of church order, clergy, hierarchy, and institution.

But, note, such a Christendom-institutional understanding of the church doesn't necessarily even require such a Spirit-animated, Spirit-gifted, Spirit-functioning community—even more tragic, the Spirit is simply displaced, except in the creeds.

In this particular Ephesians passage, the first three gifts—apostle, prophet, and evangelist—are usually dealt with lightly, almost non-essentially, while the fourth, which is the *pastor-teacher* (or "teaching shepherd," as some translate it),[17] is usually conceived of as some kind of a "clergy" (or an *ordained minister of Word and Sacrament*) figure.

Also the purpose of these four gifts is frequently looked to, in the text quoted above, as some kind of a goal, but without relating that purpose dynamically with the just-listed gifts given to the church. And, please note, the gifts are not given to individuals but, rather, to the church, i.e., they are given to the community even though exercised by individuals. The gifts don't *belong* to the individuals but to the church, for the accomplishing of its mission.

What, then, are the necessary components for *every* member of the community to function maturely and in love in the realistic dynamics of every day life in such a New Creation community? And what would be the critical components of living out their calling in the midst of an often-hostile missionary context?

I see all four of these gifts as critical and necessary *equipping gifts*—not just the pastor-teacher gift, but all four of them.[18] They are,

---

17. I am assuming with a number of commentators on this that the pastor-teacher is a hyphenated gift since there is no article "the" before the teacher, so that the text reads pastor-teachers. See Markus Barth in the Anchor Bible Series as a case in point.

18. To be sure, I am not alone in this conviction. In his book *Forgotten Ways*, Alan

to be sure, symbiotic and inter-animating. Without any one of them the people of God are short-changed, in some necessary dimension of their incarnation, as the sons and daughters of God in their daily and transformational "missionary confrontation with the world."[19] To that end, then, consider what follow as my proposals.

Apostles

The very designation *apostle* usually brings to mind the original twelve disciples, who were with Jesus. Paul will then be added and a few others whom he names as apostles along the way in his missionary journeys. The word has the flavor of "one who is sent out." Christendom has somewhat relegated *apostle* to an adjectival role, as in "the church one, holy, catholic, and apostolic" of the Nicene Creed. In that venerable creed, it means something to the effect of the church being formed by the teachings of the apostles—which in a very real sense is true. But it begs the question of why this gift from the ascended Lord to his church is listed here in such a context. Why is this gift given, and is it still germane and necessary to "all of God's people" being equipped for their daily missionary incarnation?

Face it: the first generation church had the missionary commission of Jesus Christ coded deeply in its communal DNA. It was fresh in mind—front and center. Their prayers and sacrifices and daily obedience were effectively focused in the direction of fulfilling Jesus' mandate to make disciples of every ethnic group in the world. What "sneaks up" on you in the accounts in Acts of the Apostles is that the word went *everywhere*. Day by day, many—scores, multitudes—were being added to the church. What is easily taken for granted is the spontaneous obedience of ordinary folk in the church to take the gospel of Jesus Christ and run with it.

The church was a humanly uncontrollable movement, and that movement knew no boundaries. It was *not* the special province of a few! This movement evidently took form in the continual creation of new communities, new household churches—so that we find communities of believers, quite early, in places which were a long way from Jerusalem.

Hirsch, for example, uses the code "APEPT" to speak of these equipping gifts as necessary to implement the apostolic genius in forming the church (though he sees pastor and teacher as separate gifts, and I see them as one hyphenated gift).

19. Newbigin, *Foolishness*.

The multiplicity of such communities could not possibly have been the direct result of the working of the original twelve apostles—or even of a special order of professional *apostles*!

The *gift of apostle* seems to have had to do significantly with *missionary church planting*. The church was not static or passive. New communities were being formed in homes and in many unusual contexts, in which individuals could inquire and ask questions and air their misgivings, could be taught and *discipled* to function in the ongoing expansion. In such households, or ad hoc communities, people could be equipped into being agents for organically creating yet still other communities. It also seems to have been accomplished deliberately and in a fairly short time. That is the interpretation that I see as compelling here.

What I want to propose here is that every believer was equipped by a missionary church-planter, or by one with a special capacity, or gift, of an *apostle*. This being so, it would follow—let me say it again—that every believer would then be equipped for this missional dimension of the church, namely, that of being a *missionary church-planter*. Why should that seem incredible? It would seem to flow naturally out of Jesus' commission to make disciples, teaching them to observe all that he had commanded. It meant that every member of the community had the capacity to be active in taking the gospel into unreached places, and establishing fellowships of inquirers and disciples—not church institutions, but small colonies, house churches, or intimate disciple making communities—base-camps for further missional outreach. It meant that Jesus' word about the Kingdom being like "leaven" became a reality.

Hey! New believers were not ever allowed to conceive of their calling as that of being passive participants in some religious society of those rescued. Not at all! Once you were baptized, you became part of, and were equipped to be part of, that ongoing movement. Missionary church-planters were part of the equipping ministry, and were in inter-animating relationship with the pastor-teacher, the prophet, and the evangelist. All four of these gifts were vital in equipping the community for mature missionary incarnation.

All of God's people, then, have the need to rub up against a missionary church-planter, against an *apostle*, and to get infected with the vision of reaching into those unreached pockets of people down the street, in the marketplace, in the next village, or across the world. Got it?[20]

20. The thrilling potential of this equipping in our globalized culture is that Christ's

Prophets

When living in the underside church, as many of us do, it gets almost humorous how easily we read the New Testament accounts in which, page after page, *prophets* turn up in the church with amazing regularity. Yet no one seems to pay any attention! Who were those prophets? What in the world was their function? Why were they such a prominent part of that early church? Why should prophets be of any conceivable use in equipping God's people for their work of ministry? Why are they listed here, in the Paul's epistle to the Ephesians, as equipping gifts to the church? Why is it suggested elsewhere in the New Testament that we should seek the gift of prophecy?[21]

The prophetic office in the whole of the biblical canon is fascinating. There were those persons from the early days in Israel's history who were given insights and vision by God, who were critical in keeping Israel on track (not always successfully!). My favorite would be the sons of Issachar who ". . . had understanding of the times to know what Israel ought to do."[22] That says a whole lot that we need to comprehend about our role in this present age. Our incarnation, our pilgrimage, our missionary calling, all take place in very real social and cultural environments. We are the people of *the Age to Come* who live in the midst of *this present age*. There are powerful influences at work politically, economically, environmentally, socially, culturally, traditionally, globally, and tribally. The dominion of darkness is no myth! Who is there to help us discern these influences? Who is to give us Kingdom-vision to understand whatever is the cultural context in which we live? Who are the "sons of Issachar" for our present Kingdom communities?[23]

In the field of missiology, we have often employed cultural anthropologists and cultural analysts to assist our missionary trainees in understanding such realities in whatever cross-cultural places to which they may be assigned. One perceptive professor has noted that there is really no generic Christian church, where one-size-fits-all. Every

---

followers move freely around the world in many capacities of education, business, professions of various sorts, and other capacities. This offers the possibility of sowing Kingdom seed and forming Kingdom communities in a whole other configuration than that which we ordinarily identify with missionary activity.

21. 1 Cor 14:39.
22. 1 Chr 12:32.
23. There is a strong suggestion of this necessity in 1 Corinthians 2:9–10.

Christian community exists in a very specific neighborhood, in a very real social, historical, prejudicial, and living context. Closer to home, who is to help me understand my neighbors, who operate out of different lifestyles, religions, and understandings than I? Who is going to help God's people "exegete" the culture in which they operate day by day? Who is going to equip God's people to be mature and discerning in that particular context in which they are called to be God's New Creation people—whether in Miami, Montevideo, Mumbai, or Maseru?

The prophet would be also a person with foresight, with wisdom, with knowledge of the times, but this will also necessitate that the prophet be a person of forthrightness and boldness and wisdom, which are often necessary in confronting God's people with the unpleasant scenarios that are before them (and are not always well received!).

I have always been thankful for those in the church who have helped me to understand the times and discern the culture. For a brief time, I was looked upon as one of those, because I understood something of certain generational dimensions of our culture. No one called me a prophet, but I was exercising that gift in helping others to understand. In times of social and racial turbulence in my part of the nation, there were those voices that understood both the scriptures and the culture, and so helped many of us to become reconcilers and redemptive figures in very difficult times.[24] There are those who are prophetic in many dimensions of our cultural context. According to this text, such prophetic equipping is necessary if we are to send God's people into a missionary confrontation with the realities of today (maybe ". . . lambs in the midst of wolves," as per Luke 10:3?).

The ascended Lord, by the Spirit, gives the church prophets to work, together with apostles, evangelists, and teaching pastors, to equip God's people for missionary confrontation with the world. The underside church needs to be keenly aware of this dimension of need, and acknowledge how necessary it is to have those who exercise such a gift by the Spirit.

Evangelists

Lord, have mercy! Has *this* gift ever been egregiously abused and misunderstood! We almost immediately call up the image of someone

---

24. One thinks immediately of Dr. Martin Luther King Jr. and Dr. John M. Perkins.

dramatically preaching to a large crowd, then giving an invitation to faith—replete with good music, with some emotion—well . . . you know the *shtick*. Or, maybe dutifully passing out Christian literature to unsuspecting souls. So, we need to redeem this marvelous provision from its erroneous baggage. It has little to do with what we usually identify with it. The word *evangel* itself simply means a thrilling announcement, the communicating of something astoundingly wonderful, which has happened—something that you cannot keep bottled-up inside. In the Roman Empire, the *evangelist* could be the official herald riding excitedly and breathlessly into the town square to announce a grand military victory by the Roman army. The New Testament writers adopted the term *evangelist* to speak of one who heralds that thrilling announcement of the inauguration of God's New Creation in and through Jesus Christ: "Jesus came preaching the gospel [or the *evangel*] of the Kingdom . . ."[25]

So why would this be one of the necessary gifts that the ascended Lord gives to the church for the equipping, of every one of his followers, for ministry and for mission?

Well, let's just begin by saying that God intends for his people to be thoughtful, sensitive, listening, and contagious *conversationalists* in their daily encounters with those still outside the household of faith. Among other things, it is an essential dimension of Christ's Great Commission to us to go and make disciples! That commission belongs to all of us. The gift of the evangelist is born out of an authentic compassion, which desires, with Jesus, that all should know of the love of God—of what God has done in Christ, of what the implications of that are to be.

God gives to every one of us access to others in family and neighborhood and workplace who are still captive to the darkness. Our calling is to be an expression of God's love to these folk. This calling to be evangelists has as selfless a focus on the other person as God has on us. It has components of good and sensitive listening. It has the flavor of having a thoughtful and knowledgeable grasp of what God has done, how he rescues and transforms and sets free human life—all of those pieces of the Word of Christ. We know that God comes to make broken people whole. The Spirit of Jesus Christ endows us with his own DNA of *evangelist*, and that divine nature in us can never be indifferent to what goes on in the lives of others.

25. Mark 1:14.

It is not just a spoken word, but, maybe even more, it is, as Peter describes it, that we must be "always ready to give a thoughtful answer to anyone who asks for a reason for the hope that is in you."[26] This passage, however, follows one that encourages us to live such good and exemplary Kingdom lives that those "outside"—the Gentiles, or non-religious—will be curious enough to ask! Take note, also, that this same passage reminds us that we are to give those inquiring persons our thoughtful answer with "gentleness and respect." [27]

Yes, there are those who are especially gifted at such conversational engagement, but it should be part of the furnishing that *all* of Christ's followers have. What becomes clear, then, in our Ephesians passage, is that the Lord gives this gift *to the church*, so that *all* of God's people will be freed-up and equipped and contagious in their daily engagement and conversations with others—free to be who they are called to be, free to listen to others, free to give thoughtful responses, free to be the doers of good works on behalf of others, free to invite others into the embrace of God's love in Christ, and free to respond in sometimes-hostile situations with gentleness and respect and boldness (and humor?).

Add, to such a one-on-one dimension, that the church is also, itself, in its communal dimension, to be as the demonstration of God's design for human community. As such a demonstration, it is to have a very strong evangelistic dimension within itself. Folk who have lived in the darkness, and in fractured communities or conflicted homes, have every right to be curious about these communities of faith, of harmonious loving and mutually ministering relationships—and to find their way inside in order to "scope out" what makes it so. But, if they become inquirers, they should be able to sit down over a cup of coffee and ask any member, *any one of God's people*, about his or her hope. Like, "What gives with you guys?"

Having stated (and maybe overstated?) this case for every follower of Christ being equipped for the daily opportunities of conversation in the marketplace of life, let me hasten to say that there have always been, and still are, those who are also quite skilled at heralding the gospel to large gatherings, mobs, assemblies, public meetings—and for these I am grateful. God continues to use such in many places. This doesn't detract, however, from every believer's need to be equipped to communicate with those still outside the household of God.[28]

26. 1 Pet 3:15.
27. Ibid., 3:16.
28. Just how tragically this has been neglected was demonstrated a few years ago,

So those with a *gift of evangelist* collaborate with those with the gift of prophecy, of apostle, of teaching-pastor, to equip God's people for their work of ministry, so that they grow up into maturity. In a very real sense, however, equipping God's people with this particular evangelistic capacity is a bit different. You don't learn this out of a book! I am persuaded that it is here, as with the other dimensions of our equipping, that we need mentors to be with us and show us how this is done—to teach us by *immersion* in the task. I think it requires some kind of apprenticeship. That, at least, is my own experience.

I had read lots of books on evangelism, on sharing faith, but being something of an introvert, most of what this produced in me were feelings of inadequacy, guilt, and some fearfulness. I was set free, ultimately, only in adulthood, by being on a team with a guy who really did have this gift of evangelist, and who was absolutely wonderful, hilarious, and bold in exercising it in conversation and dialogue. He loved being in the midst of those still outside of the household of faith. The more hostile the situation, the more his compassion for those folk we were encountering came to the surface. His love was mingled with marvelous humor, a keen mind, along with insights and illustrations—and real grace in hearing and fielding their questions and objections. Meanwhile, though I was part of the same evangelistic team, I was scared "spitless" and was more concerned for my own survival than for the task of turning men and women from darkness to light.[29]

In the aftermath of several evenings with this evangelistic team, watching Paul in operation at a university campus and a graduate law dormitory, the two of us were processing the evening over milkshakes, when this wonderful and exemplary evangelist and friend handed me, this introverted and frightened would-be-evangelist, some much-needed observations about my own responses in those encounters that I have never forgotten. I was set free to engage in evangelistic conversations, all of which has set me free now for many years. I don't think I could have learned this in isolation, and especially not in a church discussion group on evangelism, or by reading a book. I could multiply this illustration by

---

when a professor of evangelism in a theological school lamented to me, "How can I teach these young men and women evangelism, when they cannot even share their faith with each other over a cup of coffee?" These were those who were ostensibly to be the pastors of church institutions!

29. I'm remembering here the late Paul Little, who was Director of Evangelism for Inter-Varsity Christian Fellowship, and my much appreciated mentor.

relating other encounters where I learned from gifted evangelists in the process of the work of evangelism.[30]

Just think what it would be like if all of God's people in the church were set free and equipped for such conversational engagement in their own "Monday morning world." This is how the church reclaims its essence as a missional movement. To the necessity of equipping by the apostle, the prophet, teaching pastor, then, add that of the *evangelist.* This, I am convinced, is a significant explanation of how "the word of God grew and multiplied . . ." as recorded in Acts of the Apostles.[31]

Pastor-teachers or Teaching Shepherds

Now the question I've been waiting to ask: whatever in the world happened to the gift of the *pastor-teacher*? And comes the telling answer: If you cannot ignore or minimize such an equipping gift, then you can simply *redefine* it into something totally other than its intended purpose, and totally unrelated to the mission of God—which is exactly what has apparently happened.

Because of the filters that the Christendom hermeneutic has too often imposed upon this pastor-teacher gift by redefining it as some kind of "custodial pastor," I really don't know how to communicate how I see the place of this gift, other than to perhaps overstate my case. This gift has nothing at all to do with such a custodial role, and everything to do with the ascended Lord's passion to see all of his people formed and informed by the Word of Christ.

The teaching pastor is the one gift mentioned, in conjunction with the gifts of apostle, prophet, and evangelist, in the passage from Ephesians 4, that has been totally redefined by the Christendom church into *clergy*[32]—or into *the preacher* or *priest*, or some kind of an ecclesiastical CEO—and which becomes, then, an ecclesial authority figure. For all too much of the present church phenomenon, this position connotes a sacralized person who doesn't necessarily have much to do with equip-

---

30. If space allowed I could relate the time I was tossed into the midst of a hostile and heckling crowd on Sproul Plaza at the University of California-Berkley to engage the major profane heckler. I am still amazed at how the Spirit enabled me to make that a very fruitful encounter, and how much I learned by it. Nothing I had ever been trained to do prepared me for that moment, but being thrust out into it was one of the significant growth moments of my life.

31. Acts 12:24, etc.

32. Like "Ministers of the Word and Sacrament."

ping God's people for their own works of ministry and participation in the mission of God—as the text from Ephesians makes its purpose—in the church and in their hourly and daily lives.

The word *pastor*, actually, is a venerable word in the Scriptures and is the word *shepherd*. The Lord God is portrayed as the shepherd of Israel. The king of Israel is a shepherd-king. Jesus speaks of himself as the Good Shepherd, who lays down his life for his sheep. The word has to do with protecting and caring and guiding. Here, in Ephesians, it is linked with the function of communicating the necessary knowledge of the teachings of Christ, along with the personal caring that will equip God's people effectively in the Word of Christ, with the goal of creating mature and strong disciples who can engage in their daily ministry amidst the corrosive "winds of doctrine." It has everything to do with Christ's command to "make disciples."

In the Christendom church's better moments, there have always been those who have used their "clergy" role to be the skillful teachers of the Word of God. Please let me register that fact with much appreciation, and affirm and give thanks for those traditional church institutions whose pastor does, indeed, conscientiously form individuals and the community with Biblical knowledge. There have always been those faithful—even though quite traditional—clergy persons who saw it as their divine calling to communicate the knowledge of Christ by expositing Scripture out of their pulpits, and in classes, and one-on-one, week by week. I can only trust that I have been faithful in this responsibility.

Sadly, probably even tragically, in the North American church, the pulpit is far too often a place where sharing clever homilies has replaced its original role as the place where scriptures were exposited for the building up of the saints. Sermons are too often strings of anecdotes and illustrations loosely tied to a topic, which is, in turn, loosely related to some chosen text. Alas!

This gift emerges, in New Creation communities, in those persons who actually are the practitioners of profound and fruitful disciple-making through the communication of biblical teachings. There may be more than one in any community. These may be Bible study leaders, or teachers of classes, or those who, in any context, are formed by Scripture themselves, who are faithful to its content and understanding, and who are fruitfully bringing others to that maturity in Christ that Ephesians 4 calls for. I have seen this demonstrated in Christendom congregations all of my life. Such quiet and effective teaching shepherds are potentially the seed of our underside communities.[33]

But the transformational power is still in the Scriptures themselves. The accounts of the effectiveness of those who are expository pastor-teachers—i.e., those who "open up the biblical texts"—are fruitful and encouraging. Still, the biblical illiteracy of so many of those who profess to be followers of Jesus says to us that the gift of the teaching shepherd has been subverted into something much less and hardly related to our New Creation calling—and evidently does not equip God's people for ministry and for maturity in Christ.

A teaching shepherd cannot be a stranger, or an enigma, to God's people. Rather, he or she must be, like Paul, one who can say, with some confidence, "What you have learned and received and heard and seen in me, do; and the God of peace will be with you."[34] In its redefinition by Christendom, the pastor-teacher gift has also lost the one-on-one intimacy, the personal engagement with specific individuals, and the true intent of the caring and nurturing unto maturity that is implied in the Ephesians 4 text. It has lost its *disciple-making* component. It has also lost its inter-animation with the other three gifts of this passage. It has become altogether too disconnected from the work of making disciples who are taught to know and observe the teachings of Jesus—hence disconnected from the mission of God.

So, in the divine teleology, in the dynamics of the missional calling of the church . . . what is the purpose and essence of this pastor-teacher (or teaching shepherd) gift given to the church? What should we anticipate, or look for, or discern in its communal expression? It might serve us well to look again at the Great Commission at the end of Matthew's gospel. Do you remember (many have forgotten!) that Jesus not only instructed his followers to go and make disciples from every ethnic group in the world—but then he also gave them the specifics: " . . . teaching them to observe all that I have commanded you?" There are at least six definable sermons by Jesus just in Matthew's gospel, for starts.

Paul reminds Timothy that "all scripture is God-breathed" and *"profitable for teaching, for reproof, for correction, and for training in righ-*

---

33. In the modest congregation in which I grew up, there were three persons who formed the disciples in the Word of Christ: a dairy farmer, a teacher of the women's Bible class, and my own father who was a mechanical engineer. Clergy came and went, but these three were the ongoing teaching shepherds.

34. Phil 4:9.

teousness, that the man of God may be competent, equipped for every good work." [35] Paul's letter to the church at Colosse includes the picture of the healthy community of mutual ministry and includes this passage: "Let the word of Christ dwell among you richly, teaching and admonishing one another in all wisdom . . ."[36] Or maybe even more telling is what "sneaks up" on you in Peter's second epistle, in which he repeats how essential is *all knowledge* to our health, as those who are the recipients of God's grace and peace and of the divine nature.[37]

Question: how does this happen? Whose responsibility is it to see that *all of God's people* are thoroughly equipped in the knowledge of God, in the word of Christ, so much so that they can teach and admonish *one another*? It doesn't just happen. When folk come in from the dominion of darkness, and become part of the dominion of God's dear son, there is a lot to unlearn, first of all, and then much more to learn. It is no accident that this gift of the teaching pastor is a critical component, if, as Paul tells Timothy, God's people are to be *competent* in their lives of discipleship and in their missional faithfulness.

And, please note, this is not accomplished through one-way lectures out of a pulpit, or even in any larger class. Such public forums may be of help, but this gift is manifested more when the pastor-teacher becomes friend and mentor and model for real individuals. It is manifested when a person is engaged with those of God's people who have names and faces and stories that the pastor-teacher knows. It is manifested when they spend time together and when the mentor, the pastor-teacher, *reproduces* himself, or herself, in others, so that they can say, as Paul did, "Be imitators of me even as I also am of Christ."[38]

The vast biblical illiteracy of the church in North America is evidence that somehow this gift has been marginalized. But it is also true that, in my experience at least, where it is faithfully exercised it is usually *not* by "ordained clergy." Or to say it more bluntly: this gift is given to the church and has nothing to do with any category of *clergy*! It emerges within the community in those individuals who actually engage in such an equipping ministry. Christ's church is to be formed by the Word of

---

35. 2 Tim 3:16–17.
36. Col 3:16.
37. 2 Pet 1:2–4.
38. 1 Cor 11:1.

Christ. The gift that makes this formation into a reality rests with those who have this gifting as pastor-teachers by the Holy Spirit.[39]

In the community, this transformational relationship with the teaching shepherd is linked symbiotically with the gifts of *apostle*, *prophet*, and *evangelist* to bring *all* of God's people to maturity and fruitfulness. These gifts must be reclaimed in their integrity if the church is to fulfill its missional purpose. Absolutely! Every person baptized into the community of the New Creation must needs be equipped for the contagious role of a visible and fruitful New Creation person, and as a part of the visible and fruitful New Creation community. Only so can the church be the missionary arm of the trinitarian community. To this end, within the underside church, these gifts are to be exercised so that there becomes a leavening effect into the whole of the larger and often forgetful institution in which it resides.

HOUSEHOLD GIFTS (ROMANS 12: 3–8, 1 CORINTHIANS 12–14, 1 PETER 4: 9–11)

I need to say it once more with some amazement. It is so surprising to me, in looking for clues about the recreation of the human community as it is to be demonstrated in the church, that it is Christ's obvious provision of the dynamic presence of his own Spirit, given, for the equipping of the church, in redemptive relationships, through *gifts*, which is so easily ignored. The divine teleology, as we have noted, is for a community which makes its dwelling place in the Triune God, and in whom the Triune God makes God's own dwelling place by the Spirit.

To that end, the Spirit gives to the church those expressions of the *divine nature* that mutually minister within the relational and incarnational and very practical realities necessary for such New Creation. These gifts are given to the church primarily, and even though they are expressions of Spirit-life that pertain to all of Christ's followers, they may well be especially demonstrated in particular individuals—but even so,

---

39. A whole other dimension of the thrilling potential here is that there has been more rich and orthodox biblical scholarship in the period since World War II than in all of the history of the church previous to that. Most of this is accessible to God's people, even those of modest intellectual gifts. It is available in so many ways. I am part of a discussion class where the several teachers are those who avail themselves of rich resources and share them with the rest of us. They are causing the Word of Christ to dwell more richly in our midst. Of course there is a whole lot of disreputable, or erroneous, or heretical, or biblical junk food out there also . . . but then that is for another day.

they are not given primarily to individuals, but are given to the church as the community of God's New Creation people.

These gifts, or charisms, are not some behavioral patterns learned out of a book. They are not simply the transfer of the information about them, but they are manifested, rather, by our immersion in the *community of the Spirit*. They are given by the Spirit but also learned from *one another*. They are Spirit-given but are learned as they are observed, practiced, imitated, refined, in the context of the models and practitioners of them. They are recognized and validated by the community and as they are exercised in true love and humility. What is so regrettable about the church's common overlooking of such *pneumatic* furnishings for the community is that, when they are so exercised, there is created such a delicious and desirable communal-flesh-and-blood-culture of mutually ministering relationships. It would certainly give substance to Christ's observation that, by such expressions of his love in them, all men would know that they were his disciples.

To this end, I have termed these the *household gifts*. These are another category of Spirit-furnishings for the church. They are distinct from the missional gifts, which we looked at above, or the leadership gifts, which we shall look at next. They are also distinct from the fruits of the Spirit, which are a whole other expression of the divine nature in the people of God.

The household gifts are mentioned prominently in such passages as Romans 12, 1 Corinthians 12–14, and 1 Peter 4:9–11. Some of these gifts, not surprisingly, have an obvious supernatural component to them, such as miracles, healings, and praying in tongues. Tongues were, of course, controversial in Corinth and have become somewhat controversial in more recent Pentecostal and charismatic discussions. But praying in tongues appears to be a gift of both high praise to God, and of intercession that is given especially to some members of the community. It is one critical and essential gift and involves angelic language, by the Spirit, in its expression. It is one gift among the many that God gives for the furnishing of the New Creation community.

But this should not really surprise us since the church is the *dwelling place of God by the Spirit*. It is also true, as some commentators have observed, that each of these lists is a bit different from the others, so that it is altogether possible that we do not have anything like a comprehensive list of these gifts, but rather sample lists, or *for instance* lists. This would suggest that the ascended Lord gives special gifts as the community needs them to carry out its faithfulness in the mission of God.

We need not get lost in the debates as to whether "gifts" and "ministries" are the same role or different. My own experience is that, in a true New Creation community, there are those who exercise the gifts and are not at all self-aware that they are doing so. The rest of the community recognizes them, however. I also think that a single individual may have more than one gift, perhaps a primary and a secondary gift to the community. Some have composite gifts. Some gifts seem to be temporary, given at a time of need in the community.[40] It would seem from Scripture that a person may seek to exercise certain gifts, and God gifts men and women according to the community's needs.

Again, the apostle Paul notes that all of the gifts are given by the Spirit for the common good.[41] When the gifts become points of rivalry and spiritual "one-upmanship," then the apostle is quick to underscore that the all-determining gift, which gives validity to the rest, is the *one-another love* that must motivate and suffuse their expression. The composite of such a community of gifts is beautiful to contemplate: wisdom, knowledge, faith, healing, working of miracles, prophecy, distinguishing of spirits, tongues, interpretation of tongues, apostle, prophet, helping, administering . . . as from the Corinthian letter.

The Romans epistle offers a slightly different catalog. Here are mentioned prophecy (isn't it interesting how often prophecy crops up in the New Testament documents?), service, teaching, exhortation, the contribution of funds, leadership, and acts of mercy.[42] What an absolutely marvelous and beautiful expression of the divine provision.

The short-listing in the First Epistle of Peter, again, seems almost casual, as Peter seeks to encourage the church in a very hostile political and cultural setting. He initiates it with the encouragement to keep

---

40. There is a telling example of this in missionary annals: Amy Carmichael of Donavur, India was something of a mystic, and a very effective missionary. At a time when a plague was devastating the populace of her community, God communicated to her that he was giving her the gift of miraculous healing, which she then exercised in a most amazing way. When the plague was over, God indicated to her that the gift of miraculous healing was also withdrawn from her. This gives one much to ponder.

41. 1 Cor 12:7.

42. If it were left to me, I think I might add the gift of *facilitator* and the gift of *sparkplug* since most communities need organizers and motivators. Having said that, I think that such functions are included in the listings already in Scripture.

loving one another earnestly. Then he moves to the mutual service and stewardship of God's varied grace. He calls for open homes, or hospitality, for speaking oracles from God, for mutual service—all so that God may be glorified in such a demonstration of his divine nature in the human community!

Perhaps what is not said about God's gifting of his people, and of the New Creation culture that is to be created in such a Spirit-inhabited community . . . would be those gifts of creativity, music, artistry, poetry, industry, and stewardship of creation, which have shown up in the biblical story almost from the beginning. This is not to mention that particular hallmark of Jesus' Kingdom people: ministries to the poor and afflicted, the homeless and the unclothed, the demon possessed and sick . . . which the church in its better moments has always undertaken.

It is worth a special note here regarding "acts of mercy."[43] Given the rather overwhelming import of Jesus' teaching, in Matthew 25, about responses of his followers to the hungry, naked, prisoner, homeless, etc., . . . it would seem to be unthinkable that the Spirit's furnishing of the New Creation community would be oblivious to such ministries. I am proposing that these acts of mercy would be such an indelible expression of the life of the Spirit being sensitive to the helpless, with whom it is in contact. "In haunts of wretchedness and need . . . we catch the vision of thy tears."[44]

Such a community has the sweet *aroma of God*, and of God's New Creation all over it! Such a demonstration of New Creation community says more of the divine teleology for the church than all of the ecclesiastical institutions, hierarchical splendor, clerical hubris, incense, and liturgies that ever existed. Such an understanding of the Spirit-furnishing of God's missional community enables us to avoid being subverted by the Christendom patterns.

LEADERSHIP GIFTS

Having given clergy some pretty rough handling thus far (especially since—full disclosure—"I are one!"), let me move on to say that the New Creation is not without God-given and Spirit-provided leadership. In a

---

43. Rom 12:8.

44. From the hymn "Where Cross the Crowded Ways of Life" by Frank Mason North.

proper sense, these leadership roles are not referred to as "gifts" in the New Testament documents, yet they seem to emerge in gifted folk, who have demonstrated the edifying gifts and have been mutually acknowledged wisdom-figures in the community.

The *leadership gifts*, or provisions, emerge without explanation—and almost incidentally along the way in the New Testament documents. They also emerge out of *proven giftedness*. Let me name the three kinds of leadership that are obvious, though not easily defined: *deacon*, *elder*, and *bishop*. What were their roles? In the most basic sense, we can discern that the ascended Lord, who is building his church, knows that there is need for caring oversight and ministry within the communities.

I think it is worth observing that the communities in which these roles appeared cannot have been any kind of large and impersonal institutions, rather they were obviously small communities in which—I'll say it again—everyone had a name and a face and a story known by these leaders. After all, you cannot "Obey your leaders and submit to them"[45] . . . nor can these leaders keep "watch over your souls as those who have to give account" if they hardly know you. Again, we're talking smaller communities, maybe house churches, in which these leaders were given responsibility for oversight, by common consent, and to which the others gladly were accountable.

One of the most challenging questions ever put to me, in my role as pastor of a fairly large Presbyterian congregation, was by a rather assertive and talented young lady who assaulted me on the way into a teaching session one morning with this: "How can I submit myself to elders who don't even know my name?"

Good question.

Another caveat is that the Christendom church has unfortunately expropriated these three leadership roles and created, instead, either "clergy" or "church professionals" or corporate leaders of the ecclesial institutions. This flies in the face of what little the Scriptures teach about them. One has only to read the qualifications for these functions in the New Testament to see that they were to be models of maturity, biblical knowledge, family life, and good reputation among those still outside the community of faith—and also persons of faith, grace, and love.

I have never been a part of a Bible study group, or a house church, campus fellowship, missional team, or a small gathering of Christians, in

---

45. Heb 13:17.

which these roles did not emerge wholesomely and naturally. There are those persons who are examples of Christian discipleship, of maturity and wisdom, who are respected, and to whom the community looks for the oversight and guidance of the rest. Leadership emerges out of proven giftedness. This is not always a formal process. This seems to be what we see in the 1 Timothy 3, Titus 1, 1 Peter 5, and Hebrews 13 references to the *bishop* or *elder*. The question arises: Are these two different roles, or are they two different designations for the same role. I tend to think the latter. *Bishop* (episocopos) has to do with oversight. *Elder* (presbuteros) has to do with maturity, wisdom, and example, as well as age.

Deacon (diakonos) is a term that speaks of a ministry of service and seems to relate to those who were given responsibility to assure the church's care for the poor, its ministries of mercy, and its distribution of alms—though, again, it is never that carefully defined. But, as we noted above, the gift of acts of mercy reflects a very deep sensitivity and responsibility that existed within the community of the Kingdom of God.[46] Like the bishop and elder, the *deacon* is a model of discipleship for the community. The persons filling these needed roles are to have a good reputation even among those outside, and are to be faithful in their closest relationships, namely their own families. There is nothing impersonal or perfunctory about them. The community acknowledges their role and gladly submits to their wisdom and guidance and oversight. These persons are to willingly and gladly undertake these leadership ministries.

I acknowledge here that we have so depersonalized and institutionalized these roles that they have become known as "offices" to which we "elect" persons to fill them. Somehow, such a practice misses something of the meaning of the community of love and caring, of the nurturing and mutuality that is reflected, say, in a document such as the Ephesian epistle. I am of the opinion that persons who may not even be aware they are exercising a gift frequently exercise these functions—and persons who have not been "elected" to them. I know this is true in the underside churches that I have experienced.

---

46. We see this concern of the community for those in need in the selection of the seven men "full of wisdom and the Holy Ghost" in Acts 6, and it is often assumed that these were the first deacons, though they are never called that in the passage. But it gives us a clue as to the church's sensitivity to human need, and the fact that there were those gifted to deal with the social and economic and spiritual dimensions of such.

One notes that one of the requirements of these leaders is that they are to be given to hospitality, i.e., to have an open home. Isn't that interesting? There is warmth and personal relationship, along with the ministries of food and lodging and caring, implied in this qualification. It says something of the intimate relationships that are to be nurtured, especially by the leadership, in the New Creation community.

What one becomes aware of, in all of this understanding, is that the Lord of the Church wants his sheep—the very individual persons who make up the flock of God—to have someone responsible for them, and to whom they are accountable. We all need that. When such communities of disciples come together, there are those to whom they look for guidance and wisdom and example. People need mentors and models of what a New Creation person looks like. They need trustworthy folk who are mature, and who are wise, and knowledgeable, to give some integrity to the community and to those who compose it. In the underside church, such persons are usually easily identified by mutual affirmation of the rest, and usually with some affection.[47]

The Spirit who is the creator of the church gives gifts, or provisions, for leadership. I don't know how else to say it. Yet, in the New Testament documents and the accounts of these early missionary communities and church plants, those functions are . . . just there. They emerge by the Spirit, and the community recognizes them and responds. Our calling to be underside communities will become effective and fruitful as we reclaim this understanding of how the Spirit equips his people for community and mission.

PURPOSE OF THE GIFTS
AND THE CHURCH'S TELEOLOGY

These gifts are given, by the Spirit, primarily to the whole church, so that it can fulfill its purpose, . . . and since this equipping Spirit is the same Spirit that also inhabits every believer, there is a real sense in which all of

---

47. In my own experience, my most memorable engagement with those to whom I sensed some accountability was not within my own Presbyterian church institution, but in a summer Bible conference where there were teachers and guides who composed a Prayer Council and really felt responsible for my faithfulness and maturity in the Spirit and who, thereby, called forth from me my own sense of accountability to them. In a very real sense this was one of the most formative engagements of my life, and those guides were the persons God used to teach me the lessons of true Christian community.

these expressions (*charismata*) are to be a part of every believer's DNA, of the divine nature that is given to each believer.[48] It is only that some within the community may have one, or more, of these gifts in a unique way, and as such are able to equip others for the mission of God more effectively. When these missional gifts and household gifts become the flavor and aroma of the New Creation community, what follows will be the spontaneous growth of the church.

Pertaining to the leadership roles (gifts), Paul will even comment that those who actually *seek* the role of *overseer*, or *bishop*, are seeking a noble task, i.e., that which is essential to the community, since all of the participants need to be accountable to the community, and so one who is wise and gifted and willing to assume such responsibility in this relationship is a necessity.

The beautiful outworking of the missional gifts is that when they become the dynamic factor in the making of disciples, then every disciple will be, basically, equipped and mature in all four of these gifts: an apostle, prophet, evangelist, and pastor-teacher, with maturity in the Word of Christ, who is able to pastor others! This gives us some understanding of what Paul meant when he exhorted Timothy thusly: ". . . what you have received from me before many witnesses, entrust to faithful men and women who will be able to teach others also."[49] Or, again: "What you have learned and received and heard and seen in me, do; and the God of peace will be with you."[50] Along the way, some will emerge who express one or more of these gifts with more brilliance, or effectiveness, which will edify the others, to the praise of God . . . and, hopefully, create a more profound New Creation authenticity.

Again, all the gifts—missional, household, and leadership—are a part of the divine DNA by which the Spirit equips the church and its baptized sons and daughters for the mission of God in the practical realities of their New Creation lives. Only thus will "this gospel of the kingdom be heralded throughout the whole world, as a testimony to all nations . . ."[51]

---

48. 2 Pet 1:4.
49. 2 Tim 2:2.
50. Phil 4:9.
51. Matt 24:14.

SPECIFICS FOR THE TRAIL

Along the journey, our underside church will need to be quite self-conscious that it is communally engaged in a quiet and somewhat hidden ministry, which is the refounding of the larger church institutions by demonstrating true New Creation community and being a life-giving influence to that larger Christendom scene. Such a community, then, must itself be, in its life and inner furnishing, a creation of the Holy Spirit. This is not all that complex. In our smaller communities of faith and mission, these gifts will emerge wholesomely and fruitfully, often from the most unexpected places. Part of our ministry to each other will be to encourage the Spirit's gifts as we see them emerging in one another. The mutual responsibility and accountability that is an essential dimension of God's one-another love will ultimately come to demonstrate God's grace in furnishing his folk with the necessary ministries. And this demonstration will *leaven* the larger Christendom institutions from the *underside.* May it be so!

Trail Guide #6

Meanwhile, . . . Winter is Coming!

The last of these Trail Guides is one of urgency. The long season of the Christendom era, and of its legacy, is in its final throes. The last traces of its autumn are fading. The context of our calling is not static. All the signs of the deep winter of post-Christendom are ineluctably in evidence—probably less than a generation away . . . but even that much time is doubtful. We do not know what the next season will offer, but we can catch many clues as, even now, it is being formed by the cultural forces of post-Christendom and postmodernism (and *post*-postmodernism?). For those exiles who inhabit Christendom institutions, it is hardly a time for *laissez-faire* indifference.

It will certainly be traumatic for those still wedded to the Christendom era of the past. In the eighteenth century, Oliver Goldsmith wrote *The Deserted Village*, his poem about that similar transitional period when all of the cottage industries in the English countryside's villages were dislocated by the industrial revolution and moved into the cities. This left the quaint, rustic village of Auburn deserted, so that all the poet could do was reminisce about its former existence. The church also stood deserted and its former place in village life was but a passing memory. Ours is a similar transitional moment. The emerging future will not linger for our sentimentality.

You see, the Christendom legacy has been in place for a millennium and a half, and until very recently it has all too much formed, even held captive, our understanding of the church and its mission. Its long focus on institutions, ecclesiastical hierarchies, competing denominations, clerical dominance, church edifices inhabited by church activities and rites . . . all this, along with an attractional motivation that would somehow guarantee the population, the success, and the survival of our institutions, has totally formed this passing season.

I would propose that this probably "peaked" somewhere after World War II, when there was an orgy of building new church edifices, and a brief surge in membership and church activism. These institutions benefited by a surge of war veterans, sobered by their war experience, who came back determined to serve God by "going into the ministry." Theological schools and Bible institutes flourished and expanded. New churches were planted in the prosperous aftermath of the war. Church membership became socially acceptable, and even an expected part of the social fabric of the culture. This produced a vast population of "nominal Christians" who were loyal "church members" but somewhat oblivious to the Mission of God. Denominations became all the more hierarchical and institutionally focused. An optimistic ecumenical movement produced councils of churches. It looked like the future was unlimited for this kind of Christendom expansion.

But, somewhere in the vicinity of the 1970s, this all began to fade, cracks in the whole concept began to appear . . . and few in its leadership had eyes to see.

Ironically, it was at about that point that there erupted a brief movement that demonstrated graphically that the spiritual hunger of the emerging generation was intense, but was not being met by the church. That so-called "Jesus Revolution" is now considered by church historians to be one of the major awakenings in twentieth century church history. And . . . it took place *outside of the church*. The Jesus Revolution produced a brief generation of very creative and impassioned evangelistic expressions, especially in the "Boomer Generation."[1] Yet, it also soon became co-opted by the Christendom legacy.

Meanwhile, the culture moved further and further away from those Hebrew-Christian roots which had so significantly formed it. In its place there emerged a technological culture, and an information age culture, that has almost completely dominated the heart and mind of the populace for several generations. The (so-called) Boomer Generation was, if anything, *schizophrenic*, with one foot in its parents' Christendom cul-

---

1. One could make the case that much of the mega-church phenomenon of the past 40 years is attributable to this episode. The mega-churches seem to be attractive to the Boomer Generation, but much less so to the younger generations. All of these evaluations, of course, are generalizations. One can also follow movements of younger believers back into high-church expressions, and into monasticism.

ture, and the other in the information age culture, and not at all discerning of where that would take it (or of its own true identity).

The children of the Boomers, then, would move deeper into the technological-entertainment-information age culture, and by implication, further away from anything to do with the lingering Christian influence of their grandparents. The Generation X and the Millennial Generation are not at all that knowledgeable of, nor enamored of, that which constituted the Christendom legacy: magnificent church buildings (other than their architecture), clergy, and all of those ecclesiastical traditions and accoutrements that their grandparents found so compelling.

But, please take note: the spiritual hungering is still there. The "whited harvest field" is truly *white*. Our Lord is still passionate about his ministry to "seek and to save the lost"[2] though the church, which is the missionary arm of the Trinity. All one has to do is engage in conversation with a spectrum of those one meets along the way—in coffee houses, in pubs, in neighborhood gatherings—to find how many out there are post-Christian folk offended by the church, . . . are alternative lifestyle folk who have been condemned but not offered any good news by the church, . . . are truly *neo-pagans* creating a life without any certainties, . . . are postmodern, secular, hedonistic urban dwellers, . . . are cynics about it all, . . . or are, as per Walker Percy, "lost in the cosmos."[3]

Technology and entertainment, iPods and other electronic devices, may be an essential part of the dominant social order . . . but they don't speak to the deep questions about life's meaning and mystery that the human heart longs for. And the darkness deepens. The winter of neo-paganism grows more debilitating. Those who are "lost in the cosmos" become more numerous. The vast problems produced by economic and social injustice become more ominous. Moral, ethical, and communal values dissipate until the landscape is unrecognizable.

Yet . . . the Christendom legacy, as expressed all too much in its institutions and traditions, seems oblivious to the handwriting on the wall—to any concerns except its own ecclesiastical survival. The legacy of this past Christendom season has been the product of civic appro-

---

2. Luke 19:10.

3. Walker Percy's book *Lost In The Cosmos* came out half a century ago, but was philosophically prophetic beyond words.

bation, of generous patrons, of the blessing of the "empire"—and even those who were not a part of the church.

No longer . . .

The last generation to be significantly formed by this Christendom legacy is the generation now rapidly dying—of which I am a part. In bald terms, this is the generation that has financed the Christendom institutions for the last fifty years. What happens when they are off of the scene? The younger generation just emerging into adulthood seems not at all interested in participating in, and especially not in financing, the Christendom legacy.

Winter is coming!

Is there something to be salvaged or redeemed from this legacy? Of course there is. The question is, *what* and *how*? Knowing that the spiritual hungering is very much there, and being aware that far too many of those *outside* have been bruised and offended by the expressions of the Christendom legacy, we need to ask, what is it, that Jesus has given us, that would really be good news to a coming generation with so many garbled emotions and inarticulate longings?[4]

As the post-Christendom winter becomes more severe upon us, and the next season of our cultural sojourn is still an unknown, how are we to respond to Jesus' great passion to seek and to save the lost? Even the contextual assumptions of some kind of cultural stability for the mission of God are in radical transition. Sociologists are using words like globalization, urbanization, transnational migrations, and bilocationality to indicate a very fluid context for the church's mission.

"DECONSTRUCTING" THE CHRISTENDOM LEGACY

Meanwhile, let's see if we can *deconstruct* some of the relics of the Christendom legacy, and retrieve out of them something useful for Christ's mission to seek and to save the lost, to bind up the brokenhearted, to make all things new—something like that.

---

4. Bob Ekblad has written a compelling book entitled *Reading The Bible With The Damned*, in which he demonstrates, from actual Bible reading sessions with mostly illegal immigrants and those in prison, how utterly compelling is the biblical account in revealing a God of mercy and love to the most "effed-up" men and women. This reality translates across social and cultural lines.

In the middle of the twentieth century, there was an interesting, confusing, and very influential literary philosopher by the name of Jacques Derrida who coined the word *deconstruction*. Derrida was proposing that nothing was really knowable since every text was full of contradictions, which rendered it irreducibly complex, unstable, or impossible. It might well contain several irreconcilable and contradictory meanings. And so it went. His conclusion was that there wasn't much solid meaning in the texts and they were basically a lot of thin air. Or as some "wag" described Derrida's conclusion, "There is no there, there!"

Why do I drag that weird concept in here? Because, when you look back at our earlier Trail Guides on the teleology, cosmology, form and character, and Spirit-gifting of the New Creation community, and then look at the legacy of the Christendom era church, it should give you some pause. So much of what has been celebrated and formative in that vast and impressive display of ecclesiastical energy contradicts what is the church's *raison d'être*: its mission to incarnate the *joyous news* of the Kingdom of God, and to communicate it to all of the people groups of this world.

It is a remarkable reality that wherever the church has been fruitful in this divinely given purpose it has also been, all too often, quite *apart* from the Christendom legacy, i.e., church institutions. Rather, it has been by some spontaneous expansion that ignored the strictures of Christendom, where the gospel was "out of control" (to quote my friend Harold Kurtz). We are not the first to see the need to free the gospel from the subversion of the Christendom legacy—only we are the first to live a brief generation away from the *demise* of its essential influence in the societal culture.

Let's see if we can do a bit of *deconstruction* by way of clearing away some of the inner contradictions and subversions, and then finding what might be realized out of the rubble of the Christendom legacy that could be used in the mission of God. As we live in this *meanwhile*, between the passing and demise of the Christendom legacy and the unknown next season of the mission of God in the world, we are required to live in two essentially disparate paradigms, and hence we are required to wear "two hats."[5] Wearing one hat will require that we continue to participate in the

---

5. I am tempted to use to figures from fiction that I frequently use to help myself understand this dual role that I play in the church. One is the central figure of Disney's *Dr. Syn: The Scarecrow Of Romney Marsh*. On the one hand, Dr. Syn was a very proper

Christendom legacy, but the other hat will necessitate that we always be determining what is authentic by our understanding of the teleology of that which Jesus is building, by way of his church, and that we always be moving in that direction.

Speaking as a native of the southern United States, there is a whole lot of *ecclesiastical kudzu* that one needs to hack his or her way through, which has overgrown and hidden the essence of what Christ has called us to be and to do. Keep in mind that what we are really looking for is how to be fruitful in the current whited harvest field that our Lord has assigned us to.

BEYOND MEMBERSHIP TO DISCIPLESHIP

It should be unnecessary to make this point—but it's not. Jesus assured us that it was *he* who was building his church, not we! He also was most direct in giving us our marching orders, which was his commission to *make disciples*. Disciple-making is that coach-model-teach role, in which one meets others where they are, patiently initiates communication and introduces them to Jesus and the gospel, answers questions, "mid-wifes" them into a new life in Christ, teaches them the Word of Christ and what he has commanded us by way of life in his New Creation, prays with them, and demonstrates the new life in Christ before them . . . until they are equipped to that maturity by which they can be both salt and light in their daily lives . . . but so that they also can then make disciples of others.

Which means that the whole category of *church membership* needs to be deconstructed. Any role that allows passivity in institutional identification with the church is a blatant contradiction of that which Christ has called us to be and to do. Yet this has been all too much the pattern.

Anglican clergyman on the channel coast of England, but his other persona was a derring-do leader of a band of vigilantes seeking justice and provision for the victims of British naval policies that had deprived working families of both their men and their sustenance. These vigilantes masqueraded as scarecrows and were the bane of British naval press gangs. The other figure from fiction is the Scarlet Pimpernel, from the book of the same name, who likewise was a hero of justice, in the midst of the horrors of the French revolution, rescuing aristocrats from the guillotine. The Scarlet Pimpernel was a master of disguise and brilliant in his ability to rescue his objects out of seemingly impossible revolutionary security. In real life, he was a most unlikely British aristocrat, bored, foppish, wealthy, and vain. So I have had to assume all the demeanor of the expected role of a clergyman, while having a whole other Kingdom agenda that found so much of this Christendom legacy contradictory.

"Members" are hardly expected to be active in the work of the gospel. When church members can be indifferent to any responsibility to their part as witnesses to Christ, when they can be indifferent to the mandate to make disciples, when they can plead ignorance to that which Jesus has commanded, when they are so uninformed in the Word of Christ that they cannot teach and admonish each other in the New Creation community . . . then there is a tragic flaw. When church members can be indifferent to those in darkness in their own families, next door, in the neighborhood, in the workplace, in social networks—not to mention in the next county or across the border—then something critical is missing.

If we know that the purpose for which we are *called* by God is that we be conformed to the image of God's son,[6] then at the very heart of every Christian community should be those disciplines, and that vision of a community of disciples, growing into maturity in Christ, which, in turn, engage the context around them as salt and light, and which demonstrate the very New Creation in Christ. If this "gospel of the kingdom must be preached in all the earth for a witness,"[7] before the Lord returns, then every believer is to be a contagious and spontaneously reproducing factor in that mission.

So, when have you ever heard of Christendom church institutions with such a vision? What hinders it? What hinders it are the very Christendom structures that confine the major work of the church to "in-house" activities of worship, domination by clergy (who often are not disciple makers), and the focus on the institution's activities and successes and prestige—without reference to the mandates of Christ.

REFOUNDING CLERGY AS TEACHING SHEPHERDS AND DISCIPLE-MAKERS

In this in-between (or *meanwhile*) winter, as we pass out of the Christendom legacy and into the whatever-is-next season . . . it will be useful for those who currently are in the role of clergy to reinvent themselves as disciple makers. Sermons, liturgies, hospital visits, one-on-one conversations, and all of those occasions in which we are engaged in "pastoral duties" will become, thereby, occasions for disciple making.

6. Rom 8:29.
7. Matt 24:14.

Especially is this so in the whole questionable area of "receiving new members" into the church. Any person who presents himself, or herself, to you to become part of the church needs to know that by virtue of such identification one becomes accountable for engagement in the mission of God. There is the responsibility of discipleship written all over it. One must become conversant with the Word of Christ, and so must be equipped[8] to be mature in Christ, and so to function in one's daily ministry in a very real world.

I can testify that this is the "hat" that I have found most fulfilling in my own half-century career. A friend once described disciple-making as spending such significant time with others that you reproduce yourself in them as Christ is reproduced in you. That smacks of Paul's own teachings.[9]

And where the existing "clergy" are resistant to such, then quietly it becomes the role of the underside community to be present and to seek to engage such entrants into the disciplines of life in Christ. The underside of church history is replete with faithful folk who did exactly that. To inquirers or new members an invitation home for a meal, or an invitation for conversation to help them by way of orientation into church life, or an invitation for some one-on-one time, or a group Bible study—all of these become potentials for disciple-making and are strategic when the clergy forsake their role.

One more word: it is worthwhile for our underside cohort to encourage the professional church staff in this dimension of the mission of God. Ironically enough, many have never been encouraged in this direction, and too few theological training centers give much help in the disciple-making role.

MULTIPLYING CHURCH COMMUNITIES

Another legacy of Christendom that we need to deconstruct is the focus on building expensive and permanent church institutions. It is *never* in the biblical plan. In the New Covenant, the dwelling place of God is within his people—not within a building. The church may need a place to gather—that's okay—but the place must never become the *raison d'être*. One of the first victims of the winter that is upon us may well be

---

8. See Trail Guide #5.
9. 1 Cor 11:1, Phil 4:9, and etc.

the continued existence of large, expensive church edifices and institutions. Already one sees churches closing, church buildings up for sale, diocesan leaders closing parishes, aging congregations struggling to pay essential maintenance bills. The younger generation, if studies are worth anything, will not have a shred of interest in financing expensive "clubhouses" for church institutions. It will be no great loss.

Indeed, the essential size of the community, as we have said above (in Trail Guide # 4) must be small enough so that every person is a *person* with a name and a face and a story. It must be a context in which we can be accountable to each other, and responsible to each other for our engagement in the very real incarnation, which is our calling. This will be possible in the most informal and intimate and hospitable contexts: homes, coffee shops, parks, etc.

Meanwhile, we have these vast church buildings that are horrendously expensive. Winter is coming! As we wear our two hats in this meanwhile, we need to begin putting our hearts and minds to work on how to move out of this legacy of Christendom. How can we divest ourselves of these structures that, for most churches, are used only a few hours of the week? Of course, some lively congregations make full use of their buildings 24/7, but not many. There are many good social agencies that have found refuge in church buildings. That's fine, but that's not the reason the church has been called. When this last generation of those who are wedded to such structures, and are willing to finance them, pass from the scene (shortly), then, as we have said above and will say again, there is going to be an embarrassingly large amount of real estate on the market around the country!

Even more, such church edifices tend to be a puzzlement, or, perhaps more, a non-factor among those who are outside of the church. They are also often stumblingblocks for cynical postmodern folk. The whited harvest field is unimpressed by handsome church buildings that seem so detached from any reality known to them in that harvest field.

What we need, as we enter this deep winter of the post-Christendom period, is a passionate calling again to that very whited harvest field, to those in bondage to the darkness, to the lost who are the very ones that Jesus came to seek and to save, to the post-Christians who are offended by the church, to the alternative lifestyle population (GLBT, etc.), to the neo-pagan culture of younger adults what with their postmodern, secular, hedonistic formation, not to mention all of those well-scrubbed, upwardly mobile professionals who form a large part of our consumer society, and all of those "lost in the cosmos" folk, in whose heart of hearts there is an aching void.

Jesus came not to call church members, but sinners to repentance; he came to seek and to save the lost. And his church is to be the missionary arm of the Holy Trinity. Got it?

Meanwhile, the flavor of the incarnational communities of New Creation, again, will be effective, as these communities express a whole new, communal formation of harvesters, growing up on the underside of forgetful "harvester memorial societies." Such formations will be enclaves of hospitality, of the gospel of grace and love, of the making of disciples, of the leavening creation of new and multiplying communities, of the increasingly efficient and fruitful demonstration of salt and light.

In our meanwhile, between "what has been" and the unknown "what will be," we would do well to reclaim the very normal, leavening growth that produces incarnational communities spontaneously and healthily. In Trail Guide #5, we noted that the charismatic gift of apostle seemed to have to do with missionary church-planting. This does not at all imply creating new church institutions (though that has been the concept of the Christendom era), but rather new, mobile, flexible, edifying communities that are self-consciously part of God's great search-and-rescue mission. It is observed that probably the fastest and most fruitful growing edge of the church in the world today is in house churches. There is a proliferation of good literature on organic church growth, natural church growth, creative church growth—all of which have as their purpose that of reaching into unreached areas.[10]

It is in such intimate, lively, interactive, doxological communities of gospel that several characteristics become possible which, to the emerging generation, with its hidden spiritual hunger, will communicate warmth, hospitality, the gospel of grace and love, true community, edifying and creative times of music and of the Word of Christ, . . . and the thoughtful making of disciples. The leavening multiplication of such communities into every neighborhood and subculture should produce fruitful and increasingly effective demonstrations of the salt-and-light transformation, which our gospel of the Kingdom of God intends.

---

10. I can only commend such provocative authors such as Roland Allen, Alan Hirsh, Bob Ekblad, Reggie McNeal, Hugh Halter and Matt Smay, among others.

Such fruits of disciple making and church multiplication can, in fact, gestate in the womb of the very amnesiac Christendom church institutions we have been speaking of in this guide. Such fruits certainly do not depend upon these church institutions nor do they depend upon "clergy." What they depend upon is our faithful stewardship of that for which Christ calls us (Trail Guides #1–5).

It is such authentic communities of the Kingdom of God, of God's New Creation in Christ, that will be able to survive the deep winter of post-Christendom, and to be faithful stewards of God's gospel in the bleakest of cultural settings. The winter is upon us, but God's passion for his lost creation, which gave us his son, is never without power, nor does it ever go dormant!

What is required are those disciples who by the Spirit share God's passion for his lost creation, and who can see beyond the horizons of what has been, and move into whatever is next with creativity and anticipation. I once read a quotation that I inscribed in my journal: "The one who has the power to create *the future* has real power. The one who controls only the present controls almost nothing."[11]

I can only commend you to such a thrilling journey into the unknown future, confident that the Creator Spirit is given to equip us to engage the dominion of darkness and to be those children of light, those who are the salt of the earth, those sons and daughters of Jesus Christ, who promised never to leave us nor forsake us. It is he who sends us on such an adventure. It is in our faithfulness to such an apostolate that we become his glory.

Come Holy Spirit!

---

11. By one Cassidy Dale in *Faith Works Magazine*. That's the only reference I have to its origin.

Epilogue

Vision, Endurance, Faithfulness

WE BEGAN THIS WHOLE study with Alan's questioning of me in the coffee shop, asking me how such a church as North Park could get so "out of it" with so rich a heritage behind it. What was obvious was the struggle he was feeling between his very real affection for that venerable old congregation and his frustration, which he was experiencing because of his sense of integrity, that it had somehow forgotten what the church was all about . . . and the mindlessness of so much of it.

What Alan did not realize when he asked this of me is that he has a great company of faithful sojourners, in a multitude of traditional Christendom congregations, who also struggle continually with many such congregations that have forgotten their *raison d'être*, congregations that have diluted their message into something less than the gospel of the Kingdom of God, or which have displaced it with multiple commendable but unrelated activities—this always bewildering mixture of the "wood and hay and stubble" of merely human religion with the "silver and gold and precious stones" of the glorious gospel of Jesus Christ.

It is to such friends as Alan, and so many others whom I know and love, that I have written these studies, and introduced the vision of a ministry of *refounding the church from the underside* in the hope of being of some practical encouragement to Alan and the rest. These Trail Guides are written to give some sense of the "nuts and bolts" of purposeful ministry to those who inhabit such church communities. It has been my intention, in so doing, to reconceive the way we *think church*, and the way we *do church*, so that, while operating in the context of such churches, with all of their dependence on buildings, institutions, clergy, ecclesiastical hierarchies, . . . we can be quietly creating, from the underside, cohorts of true New Creation communities that are not dependent on such, but which are acutely self-conscious of the church's true teleology, and of its role as the communal demonstration of the gospel of the Kingdom.

And, in so doing, by God's grace, providing authentic and self-effacing cohorts of humility, love, and grace. Such cohorts, it is our prayer, will be quietly effective as leavening and refounding influences, which in God's own time will affect the whole by modeling what we have been describing in these six Trail Guides. Such underside, out-of-sight communities (which may be without ecclesiastical power or portfolio) have the potential to be a powerful instrument of the Spirit of God to bring blessing to the whole.

Our most demanding discipline, in seeking to be faithful in the context of what are, so often, church institutions afflicted by forgetfulness and spiritual darkness, will be our patient endurance. This will test our maturity. I can testify to my own impatience. But, as with our earlier illustration of a hike along the Appalachian Trail, the well-intentioned beginning doesn't guarantee our arrival at the other end without much perseverance and patience—and even suffering. So, also, when an eager gardener sows seed in the soil, he or she knows that it will be months before the fruits or blossoms are mature. We are not ever guaranteed that we will live to see the fruits of our faithfulness, but we live with the lively hope that our current abiding in Christ, and our obedient response to his word, will in God's own time bear much fruit.

"For you have need of endurance, so that when you have done the will of God you may receive what is promised."[1]

It is so with our underside communities as we seek to be those refounding influences, those witnesses to the true teleology of Christ's church, with humility and servanthood and love.

Patient endurance . . . and hope!

Our larger goal is, of course, to be instrumental in creating a *beautiful bride for the Lamb of God*.

And may the Lord be with you.

---

1. Heb 10:26.

Bibliography

Arbuckle, Gerald. *Out Of Chaos*. New York: Paulist Press, 1988.

———. *Refounding The Church*. Marynoll, NY: Orbis, 1993.

Berry, Wendell. "Christianity and the Survival of Creation." In *Sex, Economy, Freedom, and Community*. New York: Pantheon, 1993.

Boyd, Gregory. *God At War*. Downers Grove, IL: InterVarsity, 1997.

Crouch, Andy. *Culture Making: Recovering Our Creative Calling*. Downers Grove, IL: InterVarsity, 2008.

Dillard, Annie. *Teaching A Stone To Talk*. New York: Harper and Row, 1982.

Ekblad, Bob. *Reading The Bible With The Damned*. Westminster: John Knox, 2005.

Ellul, Jacques. *The Subversion Of Christianity*. Grand Rapids, MI: Eerdmans, 1986.

Gunton, Colin. *The One And The Three And The Many*. Cambridge: Cambridge University Press, 1993. Quoted in Robert Thornton Henderson, *Enchanted Community: Journey Into The Mystery Of The Church*. Eugene, OR: Wipf and Stock, 2006.

Henderson, Robert Thornton. *Enchanted Community: Journey Into The Mystery Of The Church*. Eugene, OR: Wipf and Stock, 2006.

Keesmaat, Sylvia, and Brian Walsh. *Colossians Remixed*, 134. Downers Grove, IL: InterVarsity, 2004. Quoting Walter Brueggemann.

Lohfink, Gerhard. *Jesus And Community*. Philadelphia: Fortress, 1984.

Newbigin, Leslie. *Foolishness to the Greeks: the Gospel and Western Culture*. Grand Rapids, MI: Eerdmans, 1986.

www.ingramcontent.com/pod-product-compliance
Lightning Source LLC
Chambersburg PA
CBHW071502160426
43195CB00013B/2188